BIRDS
of NEW YORK CITY
Western Long Island & Northeastern New Jersey

CHRIS C. FISHER
ANDY BEZENER

D0776033

The Publisher: Lone Pine Publishing

1901 Raymond Ave. SW, Suite C	206, 10426 – 81 Ave.	202A, 1110 Seymour St.
Renton, WA 98055	Edmonton, AB T6E 1X5	Vancouver, BC V6B 3N3
USA	Canada	Canada

Website: http://www.lonepinepublishing.com

Canadian Cataloguing in Publication Data
Fisher, Chris C. (Christopher Charles)
    Birds of New York City, Western Long Island and Northeastern New Jersey

    Includes bibliographical references and index.
    ISBN 1-55105-174-5

    1. Birds—New York Region—Identification. 2. Bird-watching—New York Region. I. Bezener, Andy. II. Title.
QL684.N7F57 1998   598'.09747'1   C98-910446-X

Senior Editor: Nancy Foulds
Project Editor: Roland Lines
Researcher: Eloise Pulos
Production Manager: David Dodge
Layout and Production: Gregory Brown
Cover Illustration: Gary Ross
Cartography: Volker Bodegom
Illustrations: Gary Ross, Ted Nordhagen, Ewa Pluciennik
Separations and Film: Elite Lithographers Co., Edmonton, Alberta
Printing: Quality Colour Press, Edmonton, Alberta

The publisher gratefully acknowledges the assistance of the Department of Canadian Heritage.

CONTENTS

ACKNOWLEDGMENTS

A book such as this is made possible by the inspired work of New York's naturalist community, whose contributions continue to advance the science of ornithology and to motivate a new generation of nature lovers.

Our thanks go to Gary Ross and Ted Nordhagen, whose illustrations have elevated the quality of this book; to the birding societies of the New York City area, which all make daily contributions to natural history; to Carole Patterson and Kindrie Grove, for their continual support; to the team at Lone Pine Publishing—Roland Lines, Nancy Foulds, Eloise Pulos, Greg Brown, Michelle Bynoe and Shane Kennedy—for their input and steering; to John Acorn and Jim Butler, for their stewardship and their remarkable passion; and to Wayne Campbell, a premier naturalist whose works have served as models of excellence.

This book would not have been possible without the assistance of Greg Butcher, the executive director of the American Birding Association. He has a lifetime of birding experience from across the Americas, and his familiarity with birding in the New York City area was an invaluable resource.

INTRODUCTION

No matter where we live, birds are a natural part of our lives. We are so used to seeing them that we often take their presence for granted, but when we take the time to notice their colors, songs and behaviors, we experience their dynamic appeal.

This book presents a brief introduction into the lives of birds. It is intended to serve as both a bird identification guide and a bird appreciation guide. Getting to know the names of birds is the first step toward getting to know birds. Once we've made contact with a species, we can better appreciate its character and mannerisms during future encounters. Over a lifetime of meetings, many birds become acquaintances, some seen daily, others not for years.

The selection of species within this book represents a balance between the familiar and the noteworthy. Many of the 126 species described in this guide are the most common species found in New York City, western Long Island and northeastern New Jersey. Others are less common, but they are noteworthy because they are important ecologically or because their particular status grants them a high profile. It would be impossible for a beginners' book such as this to comprehensively describe all the birds found in the vicinity of New York City. Furthermore, there is no one site where all the species within this book can be observed simultaneously, but most species can be viewed—at least seasonally—within a short drive (or sail) from New York City.

It is hoped that this guide will inspire novice birdwatchers into spending some time outdoors, gaining valuable experience with the local bird community. This book stresses the identity of birds, but it also attempts to bring them to life by discussing their various character traits. We often discuss these traits in human terms, because personifying a bird's character can help us to feel a bond with the birds. But the perceived links with birds should not be mistaken for actual behaviors, because our interpretations can falsely reflect the complexities of bird life.

Features of the Landscape

To the delight of the local birdwatching community, New York City offers countless birding opportunities. At any time of year, New York's beaches, backyards, forests and parks are all home to a rich variety of birds; over 400 migrating and resident species can be seen in and around the city each year. New York City is located within a major north-south bird migration path known as the Atlantic Flyway. Along this corridor, birds move north in spring and south in fall, following natural features of the landscape, such as coastal shorelines, rivers, valleys and mountains, that act as natural pathways, funneling birds along their migration routes.

The marine environment attracts thousands of birds to both beaches and shorelines each year and is largely responsible for relatively mild winter weather. Although spring and fall are usually the busiest times of year, the bays, tidal flats, beaches and estuaries around New York and Long Island are still blessed with year-round diversity. These places provide unique and valuable habitat for many birds: migrating ducks, gulls, terns and shorebirds stop here to replenish their energy supplies, moving from one productive foraging site to another; wintering birds feed on plant and animal life; and during the breeding season, many birds nest along our shorelines.

New York's broadleaf forest communities, found in our backyards and city parks, are where you will find most songbirds. These areas are often excellent places to watch and appreciate many of the interesting and colorful birds that travel through. Springtime is busy with the activity of migrating birds—oak, maple and beech communities come alive with the chattering of sparrows, nuthatches and warblers. Central Park, in Manhattan, is a wonderful place to view birdlife; not only is it enjoyed by hundreds of thousands of human visitors each year, but it also attracts thousands of migrant birds. Other parks, such as Prospect Park (Brooklyn) and Forest Park (Queens), also play an important role. Most wood warblers have spent the winter months in Central and South America and have endured an exhausting flight to reach our city. Various ponds, vast tracts of lawns, shrubs and woodland communities provide food, water and shelter for many tired and thirsty travelers.

There are many nesting residents in our area, and, in fact, the New York City region is often noted for the large number of birds that breed here. Species such as the Baltimore Oriole, Eastern Towhee and Red-eyed Vireo make New York their summer home, raising their broods in the maples, elms and shrubbery of our city parks and suburbs. Marshes and wetland areas— like those found in the Marshlands Conservancy—also host seasonal concentrations of birds and are popular nesting locations for species such

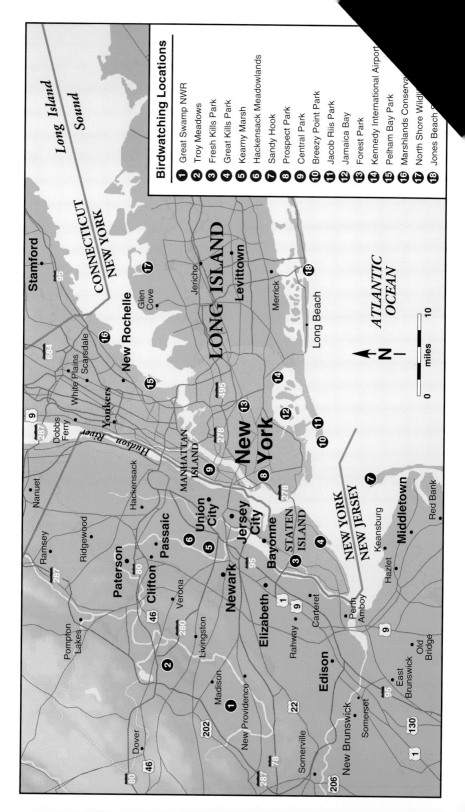

Birdwatching Locations

1. Great Swamp NWR
2. Troy Meadows
3. Fresh Kills Park
4. Great Kills Park
5. Kearny Marsh
6. Hackensack Meadowlands
7. Sandy Hook
8. Prospect Park
9. Central Park
10. Breezy Point Park
11. Jacob Riis Park
12. Jamaica Bay
13. Forest Park
14. Kennedy International Airport
15. Pelham Bay Park
16. Marshlands Conserv
17. North Shore Wildli
18. Jones Beach S

Rail, Marsh Wren and Saltmarsh Sharp-tailed Sparrow. ...y Wildlife Refuge is also an excellent summer birding ...er environment here is very productive, but there are also ...t a variety of freshwater species. The saltmarshes, tidal creeks and tidal flats of this manmade sanctuary support large concentrations of herons, gulls, egrets, terns, waterfowl and migrant passerines. During summer, more than 50 species make their nests here.

Landscaped settings are also some of the best places to become familiar with birdlife. City parks and backyards are permanent homes for the Downy Woodpecker, Blue Jay and Black-capped Chickadee, but you will also find birds that are exceptionally adapted to urban life, such as the Rock Dove, House Sparrow and European Starling. Many of the birds you will find in New York City tend to overlook the noisy lifestyle of their human counterparts and are often willing to accept their company. Backyard feeders and nest boxes are a welcome invitation for many songbirds and have successfully contributed to the reappearance of species such as the Northern Cardinal.

The Importance of Habitat

Understanding the relationships between habitats and bird species often helps identify which birds are which. Because you won't find a loon up a tree or a chickadee out at sea, habitat is an important thing to note when birdwatching.

The quality of habitat is one of the most powerful factors to influence bird distribution, and with experience you might become amazed by the predictability of some birds within a specific habitat type. The habitat icons in this book show where each species is most likely to be seen. It is important to realize that because of their migratory habits, birds are sometimes found in completely different habitats. These unexpected surprises, despite being confusing to novice birders, are among the most powerful motivations for the increasing legion of birdwatchers.

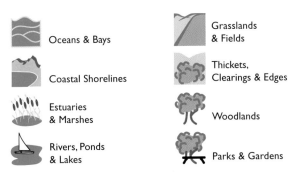

Oceans & Bays

Coastal Shorelines

Estuaries & Marshes

Rivers, Ponds & Lakes

Grasslands & Fields

Thickets, Clearings & Edges

Woodlands

Parks & Gardens

The Organization of This Book

To simplify field identification, *Birds of New York City* is organized slightly differently from other field guides, many of which use strict phylogenetic groupings. In cases where many birds from the same family are described, conventional groupings are maintained in our book. In other cases, distantly related birds that share physical and behavioral similarities are grouped together. This blend of family groupings and groups of physically similar species strives to help the novice birdwatcher identify and appreciate the birds he or she encounters.

DIVING BIRDS

loons, grebes, cormorants

These heavy-bodied birds are adapted to diving for their food. Between their underwater foraging dives, they are most frequently seen on the surface of the water. These birds could only be confused with one another or with certain diving ducks.

WETLAND WADERS

herons, ibises, rails, etc.

Although this group varies considerably in size, and represents three separate families of birds, wetland waders share similar habitat and food preferences. Some of these long-legged birds of marshes are quite common, but certain species are heard far more than they are seen.

WATERFOWL

swans, geese, ducks

Waterfowl tend to have stout bodies and webbed feet, and they are swift in flight. Although most species are associated with water, waterfowl can sometimes be seen grazing on upland sites.

VULTURES, HAWKS AND FALCONS
vultures, osprey, hawks, falcons

From forests to open country to large lakes, there are hawks and falcons hunting the skies. Their predatory look—sharp talons, hooked bills and forward-facing eyes—easily identifies members of this group. They generally forage during the day, and hawks and vultures use their broad wings to soar in thermals and updrafts.

SHOREBIRDS
plovers, sandpipers, dowitchers, etc.

Although these small, long-legged, swift-flying birds are mainly found along shores, don't be surprised to find certain species in pastures and marshy areas.

GULLS AND TERNS
gulls, terns, skimmers

Gulls are relatively large, usually light-colored birds that are frequently seen swimming, walking about in urban areas or soaring gracefully over the city. Their backs tend to be darker than their bellies, and their feet are webbed. Terns are in the same grouping as gulls, but they rarely soar and they have straight, pointed bills.

DOVES AND CUCKOOS

Both of New York's doves are easily recognizable. Rock Doves are found in all urban areas, from city parks to the downtown core, but they have many of the same physical and behavioral characteristics as the 'wilder' Mourning Doves. Cuckoos are shy birds that are seldom seen clearly as they skulk about in a world of dense shrubs—and they sound nothing like a cuckoo clock.

NOCTURNAL BIRDS
owls, nighthawks

These night hunters all have large eyes. Owls, which primarily prey on rodents, have powerful, taloned feet and strongly hooked bills. Nighthawks, which catch moths and other nocturnal insects on the wing, have extremely large mouth openings.

KINGFISHERS

The Belted Kingfisher's behavior and physical characteristics are quite unlike any other bird's in New York. It primarily hunts fish, plunging after them from the air or from an overhanging perch.

WOODPECKERS

The drumming sound as they hammer wood and their precarious foraging habits easily identify most woodpeckers. They are frequently seen in forests, clinging to trunks and chipping away bark with their straight, sturdy bills. Even when these birds cannot be seen or heard, the characteristic marks of certain species can be seen on trees in any mature forest.

HUMMINGBIRDS

The Ruby-throated Hummingbird is New York's smallest bird. Its bright colors and swift flight are very characteristic.

FLYCATCHERS

flycatchers, phoebes, kingbirds

These birds might be best identified by their foraging behavior. As their name implies, flycatchers catch insects on the wing, darting after them from a favorite perch. Many flycatchers have subdued plumage, but kingbirds are rather boldly marked.

SWIFTS AND SWALLOWS

Members of these two families are typically seen at their nest sites or in flight. Small and sleek, swallows fly gracefully in pursuit of insects. Swifts are small, dark birds with long, narrow wings and short tails, and they have a more 'mechanical' flight behavior.

JAYS AND CROWS

Many members of this family are known for their intelligence and adaptability. These birds are easily observed, and they are frequently extremely bold, teasing the animal-human barrier. They are sometimes called 'corvids,' from Corvidae, the scientific name for the family.

SMALL SONGBIRDS
chickadees, wrens, kinglets, etc.

Birds in this group are all generally smaller than a sparrow. Many of them associate with one another in mixed-species flocks, and they are commonly encountered in city parks, backyards and other wooded areas.

BLUEBIRDS AND THRUSHES
bluebirds, thrushes, robins

From the bold robin to the secretive forest thrushes, this group of beautiful singers has the finest collective voice. Although some thrushes are very familiar, others require a little experience and patience to identify.

VIREOS AND WARBLERS
vireos, warblers, redstarts, etc.

Vireos tend to dress in pale olive, whereas warblers are splashed liberally with colors. All these birds are very small, and they sing characteristic courtship songs.

MID-SIZED SONGBIRDS
tanagers, starlings, mockingbirds, etc.

The birds within this group are all sized between a sparrow and a robin. Tanagers are very colorful and sing complex, flute-like songs, and waxwings are more reserved in dress and voice. Starlings are frequently seen and heard all over New York City.

SPARROWS
towhees, sparrows, juncos

These small, often indistinct birds are predominantly brown and streaky. Their songs are often very useful in identification. Many birdwatchers discount sparrows as 'little brown birds'—towhees are colorful exceptions—but they are worthy of the extra identification effort.

BLACKBIRDS AND ORIOLES
blackbirds, cowbirds, orioles, etc.

Most of these birds are predominantly black and have relatively long tails. They are common in open areas, city parks and agricultural fields. The Eastern Meadowlark belongs in the blackbird family despite not being black and having a short tail.

FINCH-LIKE BIRDS
finches, cardinals, grosbeaks, etc.

These finches and finch-like birds are primarily adapted to feeding on seeds, and they have stout, conical bills. Many are birdfeeder regulars, and they are a familiar part of the winter scene.

Measurements

The size measurement given for each bird is an average length of the bird from the tip of its bill to the tip of its tail. It is an approximate measurement of the bird as it is seen in nature (rather than a measurement of stuffed specimens, which tend to be straighter and therefore longer).

In many situations, it is more useful to know a bird's comparative size, rather than its actual length in inches, so the 'Quick ID' for each species describes the bird's size in relation to a common, well-known bird (e.g., sparrow-sized, smaller than a robin, etc.). It must be remembered that these are general impressions of size that are influenced as much by the bulk of a bird as by its total length.

ges

ne complications to birdwatching is that many species look
n spring and summer than they do in fall and winter—they
have what are generally called *breeding* and *non-breeding* plumages—and
young birds often look quite different from their parents. This book does
not try to describe or illustrate all the different plumages of a species;
instead, it focuses on the forms that are most commonly seen in our area.
All the illustrations are of adult birds.

Abundance Charts

Accompanying each bird description is a
chart that indicates the relative abundance
of the species throughout the year. These stylized graphs offer some insight

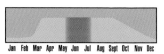

into the distribution and abundance of the birds, but they should not be
viewed as definitive—they represent a
generalized overview. There could be in-
consistencies specific to time and location, but these charts should provide
readers with a basic reference for bird
abundance and occurrence.

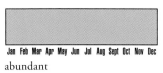

abundant

Each chart is divided into the 12 months
of the year. The pale orange that colors
the chart is an indication of abundance: the higher the color, the more
common the bird. Dark orange is used
to indicate the nesting period. The time
frame is approximate, and nesting birds
can sometimes be found both before and
after the period indicated on the chart. If
no nesting color is shown, the bird
breeds outside the New York City area,
or it visits in significant numbers only
during migration or winter.

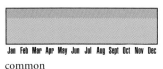

common

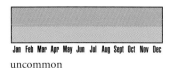

uncommon

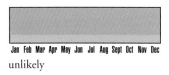

unlikely

These graphs are based on personal obser-
vations and on local references, including
those listed on p. 152.

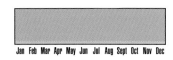

rare

BIRDS
NEW YORK CITY
Western Long Island & Northeastern New Jersey

Common Loon

Gavia immer

non-breeding

The Common Loon is a noble symbol of northern wilderness, preferring the diminishing pristine areas where birds alone quarrel over naval rights-of-way. Loons do not breed in our area, but they visit each year during migration and over winter. Around New York City, they are most often seen in their brown winter plumage as they float serenely upon the coastal waves. Great Kills Park, Jones Beach State Park, Jacob Riis Park and Sandy Hook are popular places for viewing both wintering and migrating loons.

Common Loons dive deeply and efficiently, compressing their feathers to reduce underwater drag and to decrease their buoyancy. Propelling themselves primarily with their legs, these heavy birds manage to outswim fish over short distances. Because they have solid bones (unlike most other birds) and because their legs are placed well back on their bodies for diving, Common Loons require long stretches of open water for take-off. Some loons are fatally trapped in their breeding areas by constricting ice as lakes freeze in late fall.

Similar Species: Double-crested Cormorant (p. 21) has all-black plumage and a long neck, and it usually holds its bill pointed upward when it swims. Red-throated Loon in winter plumage has white highlights on its back and lacks the dark colors on the side of the neck. Common Merganser has an orange bill and very white sides.

Jan Feb Mar Apr May Jun Jul Aug Sept Oct Nov Dec

Quick ID: larger than a duck; sexes similar; stout, sharp bill. *In flight:* hunchbacked. *Breeding:* dark green hood; black-and-white checkerboard back; fine, white 'necklace.' *Non-breeding:* sandy-brown back; light underparts.
Size: 27–33 in.

Pied-billed Grebe

Podilymbus podiceps

breeding

The small, stout, drab body of the Pied-billed Grebe seems perfectly suited to its marshy habitat, but its loud, whooping *kuk-kuk-cow-cow-cow-cowp-cowp* is a sound that seems more at home in tropical rainforests. Pied-billed Grebes can be found on most freshwater wetlands that are surrounded by cattails, bulrushes or other emergent vegetation. These diving birds are frustrating to follow as they disappear and then reappear among the water lilies and emergent plants.

Some Pied-billed Grebes remain in the New York City area during summer, sometimes nesting within view of marsh-side trails. They build floating nests, and their eggs often rest in waterlogged vegetation. Young grebes take their first swim soon after hatching, but they will instinctively clamber aboard a parent's back at the first sign of danger. Jamaica Bay, Fresh Kills Park, The Narrows along Shore Road Park and Hackensack Meadowlands in New Jersey usually produce several of these small, reclusive grebes.

Similar Species: Horned Grebe (p. 20) and Eared Grebe have light underparts. Ducks have bills that are flattened top to bottom.

Quick ID: smaller than a duck; sexes similar; all brown. *Breeding:* dark vertical band on thick, pale bill; black chin. *1st year* (summer/fall): striped brown and white.
Size: 12–14 in.

Jan Feb Mar Apr May Jun Jul Aug Sept Oct Nov Dec

Horned Grebe

Podiceps auritus

Like many water birds that winter in the New York City area, Horned Grebes lose their splendid summer plumage and assume a low-key, gray-and-white coloring. So dramatic is their transformation, that from their summer wardrobe (seen briefly in March and April before their departure) only their blood-red eyes and black back remain the same.

Horned Grebes are common in protected bays and along ocean coasts from October through April. They are commonly seen offshore from Jones Beach State Park, Jacob Riis Park and Great Kills Park. Their behavior is characteristically peppy: they leap up before neatly diving headfirst into the water.

All grebes eat feathers, a seemingly strange habit that frequently causes their digestive systems to become packed. It is thought that this behavior protects their stomachs from sharp fish bones, and it might also slow the passage of the bones through the digestive system so that more nutrients can be digested. Grebes have unusual feet: unlike the fully webbed feet of ducks, gulls, cormorants and alcids, grebes' feet have individually lobed toes.

Similar Species: Pied-billed Grebe (p. 19) has a dark neck and underparts and is almost always found in fresh water.

non-breeding

Quick ID: smaller than a duck; sexes similar. *Non-breeding:* white cheek; dark crown and upperparts; light underparts; short bill (shorter than head width); red eyes.
Size: 12¹/₂–15 in.

Jan Feb Mar Apr May Jun Jul Aug Sept Oct Nov Dec

Double-crested Cormorant

Phalacrocorax auritus

When Double-crested Cormorants are seen flying in single-file, low over the New York waterfront, the prehistoric sight hints of their ancestry. The tight, dark flocks soar and sail over the ocean until hunger or the need for rest draws them to the water's surface. It is there that cormorants seem most comfortable, disappearing beneath the surface in deep, sleek foraging dives.

Cormorants lack the ability to waterproof their feathers, so they need to dry their wings after each swim. They frequently perch on dock pilings and buoys with their wings partially spread to expose their wet feathers to the sun and the wind. It would seem to be a great disadvantage for a water bird to have to dry its wings, but the cormorant's ability to wet its feathers decreases the bird's buoyancy, making it easier for the cormorant to swim after the fish on which it preys. Sealed nostrils, a long, rudder-like tail and excellent underwater vision are other features of the cormorant's aquatic lifestyle.

breeding

Similar Species: Common Loon (p. 18) has a shorter neck and is more stout overall. Great Cormorant is larger and has a white chin strap and (during the breeding season) white flank patches.

Quick ID: goose-sized; sexes similar; all black; long tail; long neck. *In flight:* kinked neck; rapid wingbeats. *Breeding:* bright orange throat pouch; black plumes streaming back from eyebrows (seen only at close range). *1st year:* brown overall; pale neck and breast.
Size: 30–35 in.

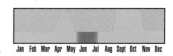

Jan Feb Mar Apr May Jun Jul Aug Sept Oct Nov Dec

Great Blue Heron

Ardea herodias

Long before Lady Liberty graced our harbor waters, the Great Blue Heron was regaling shorelines with its statuesque beauty. It often stands motionless as it surveys the calm waters, its graceful lines blending naturally with the grasses and cattails of wetlands. All herons have specialized vertebrae that enable the neck to fold back over itself. The S-shaped neck, seen in flight, identifies all members of this wading family.

Hunting herons space themselves out evenly in favorite hunting spots, and they will strike out suddenly at prey below the water's surface. In flight, their lazy wingbeats slowly but effortlessly carry them up to their nests. These herons nest communally high in trees, building bulky stick nests that are easily seen along wooded swamps and beaver ponds north of New York City and at Great Swamp National Wildlife Refuge in New Jersey. Although they do not breed in the city, migrating and non-breeding birds can often be seen strolling elegantly through the shallows of Jamaica Bay, Fresh Kills Park and even Rowboat Lake in Central Park.

Similar Species: Great (p. 23), Cattle and Snowy egrets are similar to the Great Blue Heron in build, but they are all white. Black-crowned Night-Heron has a black cap and back. Yellow-crowned Night-Heron has a black-and-white head and an all-gray body. Little Blue Heron is half the size and has a grayish bill.

Quick ID: very large heron; sexes similar; gray-blue plumage; long, dagger-like, yellow bill. *In flight:* eagle-sized wingspan; head folded back; legs held straight back.
Size: 48–52 in.

Jan Feb Mar Apr May Jun Jul Aug Sept Oct Nov Dec

Great Egret

Ardea alba

The silky silhouette of the Great Egret graces many marshes, tidal flats and estuaries in the New York City area. It stalks shallow waters for fish, amphibians and sometimes small birds and mammals. The diligence and patience it displays while hunting contrasts with its lightning-quick, spearing thrust. At dusk, waves of these ghostly birds trace their way back to their communal nesting and roosting sites, which are usually in areas isolated from humans. Nesting can be viewed at Jamaica Bay Wildlife Refuge, Jones Beach State Park and Shooter's Island. Great Egrets regularly visit Hackensack Meadowlands in New Jersey in late summer and early fall.

From their arrival in March through late spring, the Great Egret's form is enhanced by the presence of 'nuptial plumes' that flare from its lower neck and back. Earlier this century, people coveted these feathers for fashion accessories, and Great Egret populations were decimated before legislation was enacted to protect them.

Similar Species: Snowy Egret is smaller and has yellow feet. Cattle Egret is smaller and has a shorter bill and light-colored feet. Immature Little Blue Heron is much smaller and has a grayish, black-tipped bill and greenish legs.

breeding

Quick ID: large heron; sexes similar; all-white plumage; long, yellow bill; black legs and feet.
Breeding: long white plumes from base of neck and back; green lore.
Size: 38 in.

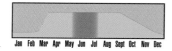

Jan Feb Mar Apr May Jun Jul Aug Sept Oct Nov Dec

Green Heron

Butorides virescens

This crow-sized heron is far less conspicuous than its Great Blue cousin. The Green Heron prefers to hunt for frogs and small fish in shallow, weedy wetlands, where it is often seen perched just above the water's surface. By searching the shallow, shady, overgrown, marshy edges of inland ponds and coastal shorelines, New York City birders can sometimes get a prolonged view of this otherwise reclusive bird. Great Swamp National Wildlife Refuge in New Jersey also has a breeding population of Green Herons.

The Green Heron often uses all of its small stature to hunt over a favorite site. With its bright yellow or orange feet clasping a branch or reed, this small heron stretches nearly horizontally over the water, its pose rigid and unchanging, until a fish swims into range. Like a taut bowstring, the tension mounts until the heron chooses to fire. Lunging its entire body at its prey, the heron is often soaked to the shoulders.

Similar Species: American Bittern is larger, is heavily streaked and lacks the dark crown. Least Bittern shows a contrast of darker colors with buffy-orange. Little Blue Heron lacks the chestnut throat.

Jan Feb Mar Apr May Jun Jul Aug Sept Oct Nov Dec

Quick ID: small, stubby, crow-sized heron; sexes similar; short legs; glossy green back; chestnut throat; dark cap. *Breeding male:* orange legs. *Immature:* less colorful; heavily streaked.
Size: 18–21 in.

Glossy Ibis

Plegadis falcinellus

The exotic look of this unusual, long-legged bird hints of its distant, West African origins. The Glossy Ibis is thought to have long ago crossed the Atlantic Ocean to the Caribbean using the powerful trade winds, and it has since expanded its natural breeding range north into New York. The Glossy Ibis is abundant from late April to mid-September in the marshy habitats of Jamaica Bay, Jones Beach and similar locations throughout southwestern Long Island. In late summer and early fall, these birds visit Hackensack Meadowlands and Kearny Marsh in New Jersey.

Quietly watch for the awkward maneuvers of a mating pair as they precariously balance their bulky platform nest of sticks and vegetation on the top of a small tree or shrub. The long, sickle-shaped bill of the Glossy Ibis is a precision instrument skillfully used to probe marshland mud and waters for a variety of small prey, including insects, snails, crabs, crayfish, frogs and small fish.

Similar Species: All herons have straight bills. Whimbrel is brown, not glossy chestnut.

breeding

Quick ID: small heron–sized; sexes similar; long, downcurved bill; long legs; chestnut neck and body; glossy green-and-purple wings, tail and face.
Size: 23 in.

Jan Feb Mar Apr May Jun Jul Aug Sept Oct Nov Dec

Clapper Rail

Rallus longirostris

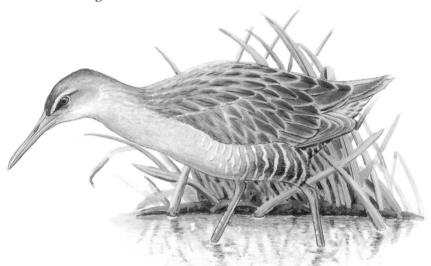

Although the Clapper Rail is large and noisy, its plumage and subtle movements usually keep it hidden from view. It is only when high tides flood the marshes that the secretive Clapper can be seen with any regularity. The high waters drive the birds out of their cattail stems above the tide. New York City residents who retreat to Jamaica Bay or other saltwater marshes in southern Long Island can experience the loud, clattering calls of rails roaring from salty marsh hideaways at twilight.

Elsewhere, the Clapper Rail is increasingly becoming endangered as development swallows up or pollutes coastal marsh habitat. The increased protection of our coastal marsh habitats has thus far prevented our Clapper Rails from suffering a similar fate.

Similar Species: Virginia Rail is much smaller and has gray cheeks. King Rail has a clearer contrast between its brighter, light and dark colors and prefers freshwater habitats.

Jan Feb Mar Apr May Jun Jul Aug Sept Oct Nov Dec

Quick ID: chicken-sized; sexes similar; stout, dark brown body; long, slightly downcurved bill; gray-and-white barring on flanks; short, cocked tail; white undertail; gray-and-black streaks on back.
Size: 14–16 in.

American Coot

Fulica americana

The American Coot is a curious mix of comedy and confusion: it seems to have been made up of bits and pieces leftover from other birds. It has the lobed toes of a grebe, the bill of a chicken and the body shape and swimming habits of a duck, but it is not remotely related to any of these species—its closest cousins are rails and cranes. American Coots dabble and dive in water and forage on land, and they eat both plant and animal matter. They are a rare, year-round addition to fresh- and saltwater marshes in the New York City area.

These loud, grouchy birds are usually seen chugging along in wetlands, frequently entering into short-lived disputes with neighboring coots. American Coots appear comical when they swim: their heads bob in time with their paddling feet, and as a coot's swimming speed increases, so does the back-and-forth motion of its head. At peak speed, this motion seems to disorient the coot, so it prefers to run, flap and splash to the other side of the wetland.

Similar Species: All ducks and grebes generally lack the uniform black color and the all-white bill. Pied-billed Grebe (p. 19) is brown.

Quick ID: smaller than a duck; sexes similar; black body; white bill; red forehead shield; short tail; long legs; lobed feet; white undertail coverts.
Size: 14–16 in.

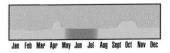

Jan Feb Mar Apr May Jun Jul Aug Sept Oct Nov Dec

Mute Swan

Cygnus olor

Gracing the waters of New York City and Long Island, the Mute Swan looks and acts like a movie star. Its romantic composure, its beautiful, silken wing plumes and the warm accents of black and orange on its head grant this bird a regal stature. The Mute Swan has a very nasty side, however, and it pinches and pecks at any individual—bird or human—that dares to challenge its space.

This Eurasian native was introduced to estate ponds and city parks throughout the eastern United States during the late 1800s, and it quickly adapted to its New World home. A non-migrant, the Mute Swan appears to be a thriving summer breeder and winter resident in sheltered coastal waters and freshwater wetlands throughout the region. As with so many introduced animals, the Mute Swan's population is expanding, and in some cases the Mute Swan is displacing native New York waterfowl species and over-grazing vegetation locally.

Similar Species: Tundra Swan has an all-black bill that lacks a knob, and it holds its neck straighter.

Jan Feb Mar Apr May Jun Jul Aug Sept Oct Nov Dec

Quick ID: larger than a goose; sexes similar; often swims with wings slightly raised; thick neck; black feet. *Adult:* all-white body; orange or pink bill with black knob at base. *Immature:* grayish-brownish body; all-dark bill. **Size:** 52–60 in. (male slightly larger).

Canada Goose

Branta canadensis

Most flocks of Canada Geese in city parks and golf courses show little concern for their human neighbors. These urban geese seem to think nothing of creating a traffic jam, blocking a fairway or dining on a lawn. Their love of manicured parks and gardens and the lack of predators have created somewhat of a population explosion in many parts of New York City and Long Island. From early April to mid-June, Central, Prospect and Pelham Bay parks are all great places to find pairs of Canada Geese leading their obedient, downy yellow goslings down to the water's edge for their first swim.

Breeding pairs of Canada Geese are regal in appearance, and their loyalty is legendary—they mate for life, and it's common for a mate to stay at the side of a fallen partner. The geese that are permanent residents may be dominant to the migratory birds that migrate through New York. Our local birds' territoriality and aggression towards the migrants parallels the reputation earned by many a New Yorker.

Similar Species: Brant (p. 30) lacks the white cheek, has a black upper breast and has a faint white 'necklace' across the front of the throat.

Quick ID: large goose; sexes similar; white cheek; black head and neck; brown body; white undertail coverts.
Size: 35–42 in.

Jan Feb Mar Apr May Jun Jul Aug Sept Oct Nov Dec

Brant

Branta bernicla

The eelgrass beds that spread out along the Atlantic Coast provide ideal winter vacation spots for this small, dark goose. Thousands of Brant winter along the south shore of Long Island each year, splitting their time between the water, where they feed on aquatic vegetation, and dry grasslands (lawns and golf courses), where they graze like Canada Geese. If you scan the shorelines of Jones Beach or Jamaica Bay from December to April, you will often see large rafts of these handsome waterfowl.

Brant leave the New York City and Long Island area in May to migrate to their breeding grounds on the Arctic tundra. They do not fly in tight V formations like Canada Geese; instead, their flocks fly in wavy lines that frequently alternate between balling up and stretching out. If you encounter a flock feeding or resting along our shorelines, view the birds' delicate, lace-like throat markings and social behavior from a distance—disrupted, they will often shuffle into the water and away from their important daily activities.

Similar Species: Canada Goose (p. 29) is larger and has white cheeks.

Jan Feb Mar Apr May Jun Jul Aug Sept Oct Nov Dec

Quick ID: small goose; sexes similar; dark overall; no cheek patch; faint white 'necklace'; white undertail coverts.
Size: 23–26 in.

Wood Duck

Aix sponsa

The male Wood Duck is one of the most colorful waterfowl in North America. Books, magazines, postcards and calendars routinely celebrate its beauty. No other duck can match this New York City resident's colorful, iridescent and intricate plumage.

Wood Ducks nest in natural tree cavities or in nest boxes along ponds on Staten Island, in Nassau and Westchester county parks and at Great Swamp National Wildlife Refuge. The nests are usually found near water, where they can be up to 60 feet high in trees. The cavities themselves can contain as many as 12 eggs in a single feather-lined nest. Soon after hatching, the ducklings take the ultimate 'leap of faith,' jumping to the ground from their nest. These cottonballs of down rarely injure themselves and, once composed, waddle off to the nearest wetland, where they complete their development. Following breeding, Wood Ducks are often found in the North Shore Wildlife Sanctuary, where the males molt and lose all of their striking breeding plumage.

Similar Species: Hooded Merganser has a white patch on its crest and a slim bill.

Quick ID: small duck. *Male:* glossy green head; crest slicked back from crown; white chin and throat; chestnut breast spotted white; white shoulder slash; golden sides; dark back and hindquarters. *Female:* white teardrop eye patch; mottled brown breast streaked white; brown-gray upperparts; white belly.
Size: 19–20¹/₂ in.

Jan Feb Mar Apr May Jun Jul Aug Sept Oct Nov Dec

American Wigeon

Anas americana

During the winter months, American Wigeons can easily be found and identified on saltwater marshes along the coast and on freshwater inland ponds. At that time of year, flocks of wigeons are commonly seen waddling across lawns and floating offshore on Jamaica Bay and other local waterways. The white top and gray sides of the male American Wigeon's head look somewhat like a balding scalp, while the nasal *wee-he-he-he* calls sound remarkably like the squeaks of a squeezed rubber ducky.

With the exception of the occasional brutal winter storm, the relatively mild coastal climate usually makes life easy and comfortable for these and many other species of overwintering waterfowl. Robed in a waterproof coat of finely oiled feathers, wigeons are free to frolic among unfrozen waters in search of palatable aquatic vegetation. Most American Wigeons prefer to spend their summers nesting far north of our area.

Similar Species: Green-winged Teal (p. 37) is smaller, has a white shoulder slash and has a rusty head with a green swipe. Eurasian Wigeon has a reddish head, a gray back and gray sides.

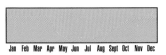

Jan Feb Mar Apr May Jun Jul Aug Sept Oct Nov Dec

Quick ID: mid-sized duck; cinnamon breast and flanks; white belly; gray, black-tipped bill; green speculum. *Male:* white forehead; green swipe running back from eye. *Female:* no distinct colors on head.
Size: 18–21 in.

American Black Duck

Anas rubripes

Among the flocks of waterfowl wintering on open waters in the New York City area, you will find the plain-looking American Black Duck. Like a dark version of the familiar Mallard (except for its silver wing linings, dark orange feet and purple wing patch), the American Black Duck is the classic duck of eastern North America, and a healthy population resides in our area. American Black Ducks are more common on salt and brackish water; Mallards are more dominant on freshwater ponds.

Unfortunately, the eastern expansion of Mallards has come at the expense of this dark dabbler. As its green-headed cousin spread into our area, the American Black Duck hybridized with the Mallard. Some biologists are concerned about this genetic watering down of pure American Black Duck stock, and the future stability of the species is unknown. Habitat loss and the degradation of wetlands in general have further contributed to the decline of this bird. Although it is plain in appearance, the state of the American Black Duck's future increases the profile of this East Coast specialty in the eyes and minds of conservation-oriented naturalists.

Similar Species: Mallard (p. 34) has an overall lighter body plumage and a blue speculum bordered with white, and the male has a green head. Gadwall lacks the yellow bill and has a black-and-white speculum.

Quick ID: large duck; dark blackish-brown body; light brown-gray head and neck; bright orange feet. *Male:* yellow bill. *Female:* dull green bill spotted with black. *In flight:* silver-lined wings.
Size: 22–24 in.

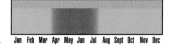

Jan Feb Mar Apr May Jun Jul Aug Sept Oct Nov Dec

Mallard

Anas platyrhynchos

The Mallard is the classic duck of freshwater marshes and ponds—the male's iridescent green head and chestnut breast are symbolic of wetland habitat. This large duck is commonly seen feeding in city parks and local ponds, tipping bottoms-up in the water or grazing confidently on land. With their legs positioned under the middle part of their bodies, Mallards walk easily, and they can spring straight out of water without a running start.

Mallards are the most common duck in North America (and the Northern Hemisphere), and they are easily seen in New York City every day of the year. During winter, Mallards are seen mixed with flocks of ducks on open water and occasionally on coastal bays and estuaries. Because several duck species often band together in these loose flocks, birdwatchers habitually scan these groups to test their identification skills. Mallards (like all ducks) molt several times a year, so remember that the distinctive green head of the male Mallard occasionally loses some of its pizzazz.

Similar Species: Female resembles many other female dabbling ducks, but look for the iridescent blue speculum, bordered by white on both sides, and her close association with the distinctive male. Male Northern Shoveler (p. 36) has a green head, a white breast, chestnut flanks and a much longer bill.

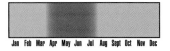

Jan Feb Mar Apr May Jun Jul Aug Sept Oct Nov Dec

Quick ID: large duck; bright orange feet; iridescent blue (or purple in male) speculum bordered by white. *Male:* iridescent green head; bright yellow bill; chestnut breast; white flanks. *Female:* mottled brown overall; bright orange bill marked with black.
Size: 22–26 in.

Blue-winged Teal

Anas discors

The male Blue-winged Teal has a thin, white crescent on his cheek and a steel blue head to match his inner wing patches. These small ducks are extremely swift flyers, which frustrates their many predators. Their sleek design and rapid wingbeats enable them to swerve even at great speeds, and also give the small ducks the accuracy to make perfectly placed landings.

Unlike many of the larger pond ducks, which overwinter in the United States, most teals migrate to Central and South America. For this reason, the Blue-winged Teal is often the last duck to arrive in New York City during spring and the first to leave in fall, usually by the end of September. Although your best chance of seeing a Blue-winged Teal is during spring or fall migration, these colorful ducks will certainly be encountered by observant visitors during the summer months when New York City–area wetlands come alive with lively courtship antics.

Similar Species: Female is easily confused with other female dabbling ducks.

Quick ID: very small duck; blue forewing; green speculum. *Male:* steel blue head; white crescent on cheek. *Female:* small; plain; yellow legs.
Size: 14–16 in.

Jan Feb Mar Apr May Jun Jul Aug Sept Oct Nov Dec

Northern Shoveler

Anas clypeata

♂ ♀

The Northern Shoveler's shovel-like bill stands out among the dabbling duck brigade. The comb-like structures along the bill's edges and its broad, flat shape allow the shoveler to strain small plants and invertebrates from the water's surface or from muddy substrates. A few Northern Shovelers breed at Jamaica Bay each year, but most of the shovelers seen in the winter breed on inland ponds far to the north.

Many novice New York birders become interested in birds because they realize the great variety of ducks found in and around the city. Some ducks, like the Northern Shoveler, are dabblers that prefer shallow water. They are not opposed to roaming around on land and they can lift straight off the water like a helicopter. Many other ducks in the New York City and Long Island area are divers that are found on saltwater bays, large inland lakes and reservoirs. They are routinely seen running across the water to gain enough speed for flight. Separating the divers from the dabblers is a first step into the wondrous world of waterfowl.

Similar Species: Mallard (p. 34) and all other dabbling ducks lack the combination of a large bill, a white breast and chestnut sides.

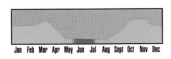

Jan Feb Mar Apr May Jun Jul Aug Sept Oct Nov Dec

Quick ID: mid-sized duck; large bill (longer than head width). *Male:* green head; white breast; chestnut sides. *Female:* mottled brown overall.
Size: 18–20 in.

Green-winged Teal

Anas crecca

With few places in the New York City area providing the densely vegetated pond habitats needed by this dainty duck to produce and raise young successfully, the Green-winged Teal is at best an uncommon summer resident and breeder. Eager birders are most likely to see the Green-winged Teal during migration in April and September as it briefly stops in local ponds and marshes to replenish its energy reserves. This attractive dabbler is also an uncommon winter resident, often found feeding in shallow, unfrozen tidal marshes and estuaries.

These small ducks prefer calm waters, where they often shun the company of larger waterfowl and remain with their own kind. When Green-winged Teals take to the air, they are among the fastest of ducks, showing their green inner wing patches amid a blur of wingbeats.

Similar Species: Blue-winged Teal (p. 35) has a blue wing patch and lacks the white undertail coverts, and the male has a steel blue head and a white crescent on the face. American Wigeon (p. 32) has a white forehead and a black hind end.

Quick ID: small duck; green wing patch.
Male: chestnut head; green swipe trailing from eye; white, vertical shoulder slash; gray body.
Female: mottled brown overall.
Size: 14–16 in.

Jan Feb Mar Apr May Jun Jul Aug Sept Oct Nov Dec

Canvasback

Aythya valisineria

Although most Canvasbacks choose to spend their winters in warmer southern climates, each year several hundred of these birds make their winter home off the coast of Long Island, majestically swimming in open waters with their bills held high. Canvasbacks are ducks of the deep water, and they acquire their vegetarian diet in well-spaced dives. Birders can easily identify the stately Canvasback at a distance. Its distinctive profile results from the apparent lack of a forehead—the dark bill appears to run straight up to the top of the bird's head, giving the Canvasback sleek, hydrodynamic-looking contours.

The Redhead is a closely related duck that is very similar in appearance. Like the male Canvasback's head, the male Redhead's head is—you guessed it—red, but its back is gray instead of white. Also, the Redhead has a noticeable forehead, just like it is wearing a ball cap. Both the Canvasback and the Redhead leave the New York City and Long Island area in late March to early April to raise their young on Great Plains wetlands.

Similar Species: Greater Scaup (p. 39) and Lesser Scaup lack the chestnut head and the sloping forehead. Redhead lacks the sloping forehead and has a black-tipped, gray bill and a gray back.

Jan Feb Mar Apr May Jun Jul Aug Sept Oct Nov Dec

Quick ID: large duck; sloping, blackish bill and forehead. *Male:* canvas white back; chestnut head; black breast and hindquarters. *Female:* brown head and neck; light gray body.
Size: 19–22 in.

Greater Scaup

Aythya marila

The Greater Scaup is the Oreo cookie of the coastal ducks—black at both ends and white in the middle. It is a diving duck that prefers deep, open water, and during winter hundreds of them can be seen plying the waters off Long Island's southern coast and in western Long Island Sound.

Most ducks seen in deep water are diving ducks, while those seen on shallow ponds or walking on land tend to be dabbling ducks. Diving ducks have smaller wings, which help them underwater but make for difficult take-offs and landings. When a duck scoots across the water in an attempt to get airborne, even a first-time birder can tell it's a diver. Divers' legs are placed well back on their bodies—an advantage for underwater swimming but not for easy walking. All ducks are front-heavy, so for diving ducks to stand, they must raise their front ends high to maintain balance.

Similar Species: Common Goldeneye (p. 42) lacks the black breast. Lesser Scaup has a purplish tinge to its head. Ring-necked Duck has a black back and a white shoulder slash, and both species tend to occur in smaller flocks on fresh water.

Quick ID: mid-sized duck. *Male:* dark, rounded head with hints of green; black breast and hindquarters; grayish-white sides and upperparts. *Female:* dark brown; well-defined white patch at base of bill.
Size: 18 in.

Jan Feb Mar Apr May Jun Jul Aug Sept Oct Nov Dec

White-winged Scoter

Melanitta fusca

As White-winged Scoters race across choppy winter seas, their flapping wings reveal this bird's key diagnostic feature—a white inner wing patch that strikes a sharp contrast with the bird's otherwise all-black plumage and the dark waters.

Scoters are heavy-bodied ducks that use both their feet and their partially spread wings in deep foraging dives, which can last up to one minute or so. These large ducks form rafts on offshore waters, where they dive for snails, mussels, clams and crustaceans. The gizzards of scoters are exceptionally strong, and they can easily grind these hard-shell invertebrates into digestible matter.

Look for White-winged Scoters and their relatives, Surf Scoters and Black Scoters, floating in mixed-species rafts off the shores of Jones Beach, Breezy Point or Crookes Point in Great Kills Park.

Similar Species: Surf Scoter lacks the white wing patches, and the male has a white forehead and nape. Black Scoter is all black, with no white on its wings or head, and it has a bulbous, orange bill.

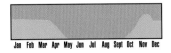

Jan Feb Mar Apr May Jun Jul Aug Sept Oct Nov Dec

Quick ID: large, stocky duck; white wing patch; large bill; sloping forehead; base of bill is fully feathered. *Male:* black overall; white eye patch. *Female:* brown overall; gray-brown bill; light patches on cheek and ear.
Size: 20–23 in.

Bufflehead

Bucephala albeola

The small, 'baby-faced' Bufflehead is perhaps the 'cutest' of New York City's ducks; its simple plumage and rotund physique bring to mind a child's stuffed toy. During fall migration and winter, these charming birds are commonly seen in freshwater ponds and on the offshore ocean waves of Jamaica Bay, Jones Beach and Pelham Bay.

Because ducks spend most of their lives dripping with water, preening is an important behavior. At the base of the tail of most birds lies the preen (uropygial) gland, which secretes a viscous liquid that inhibits bacterial growth and waterproofs and conditions the feathers. After gently squeezing the preen gland with its bill, a bird can spread the secretion methodically over most of its body, an essential and commonly observed practice to revitalize precious feathers. Because sun, wind and salt water damage feathers, it is understandable that birds spend so much time in the preening and maintenance of their feathers.

Similar Species: Male Common Goldeneye (p. 42) is larger and lacks the white, unbordered triangle behind the eye. Male Hooded Merganser has brownish sides, a white slash by its shoulder and a black outline to its white crest.

Quick ID: small duck; round body. *Male:* white triangle on back of otherwise dark head; white body; dark back. *Female:* dirty brown; small white cheek patch.
Size: 13–15 in.

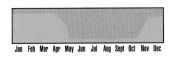

Jan Feb Mar Apr May Jun Jul Aug Sept Oct Nov Dec

Common Goldeneye
Bucephala clangula

Although Common Goldeneyes don't breed in the New York City area, they are locally common from late fall right up to their spring migration. Their courtship antics, staged on Jamaica Bay, the Hudson River and just about every other large waterbody from winter through spring, reinforce a pair's bond prior to their migration to northern woodland lakes.

The courtship display of this widespread duck is one of nature's best slapstick routines. The spry male goldeneye rapidly arches his large green head back until his bill points skyward, producing a seemingly painful *kraaaagh*. Completely unaffected by this chiropractic wonder, he performs this ritual non-stop to mainly disinterested females. The male continually escalates his spring performance, creating a comedic scene that is most appreciated by birdwatchers.

Similar Species: Bufflehead (p. 41) and Hooded Merganser lack the round, white cheek patch.

Jan Feb Mar Apr May Jun Jul Aug Sept Oct Nov Dec

Quick ID: mid-sized duck. *Male:* large, dark green to black head; round, white cheek patch; white body; black back streaked with white. *Female:* chocolate brown hood; sandy-colored body.
Size: 17–19 in.

Red-breasted Merganser

Mergus serrator

As warm spring weather arrives in the New York City area, Red-breasted Mergansers congregate along the coast, initiating their courting rituals here before their final push north. Sporting punk-like, slicked crests, the males ride the waters with their necks lowered under the surface. With their mid-points submerged, they stare eerily with their wild red eyes, evaluating the females' responses to their actions.

Large, gregarious flocks of Red-breasted Mergansers move up the coast or begin their inland journey during migration. Unlike the Common Merganser, however, they tend to retreat to coastal waters for the winter. During their stay in our area, their quick 'fly bys,' which flash white inner wing patches, are commonly seen off Jacob Riis Park, Jones Beach and Conference House Park.

Similar Species: Other large ducks and Common Loon (p. 18) lack the combination of a green head, orange bill, orange feet and red breast. Male Common Merganser lacks the rusty breast and has white underparts, and the female has a well-defined, reddish-brown hood.

Quick ID: large duck; gray body. *Male:* well-defined, dark green hood; punk-like crest; streaked, rusty breast; white collar; brilliant orange bill and feet; black spinal streak. *Female:* rusty hood blending into white breast.
Size: 21–25 in.

Jan Feb Mar Apr May Jun Jul Aug Sept Oct Nov Dec

Ruddy Duck

Oxyura jamaicensis

breeding

Celebrated for their comical courting displays, cheeky male Ruddy Ducks are renowned as the clowns of freshwater wetlands. Males energetically paddle around their breeding wetlands, displaying with great vigor and beating their breasts with their bright blue beaks. The *plap, plap, plap-plap-plap* sound of their display speeds up until its climax: a spasmodic jerk and sputter. The Ruddy Duck's winter demeanor contrasts sharply with its summer habits. During winter, the drably plumaged males lack the courting energy and colors of summer.

New Yorkers are blessed with the opportunity to enjoy Ruddy Ducks year-round. These stiff-tailed diving ducks are reliable breeders at Hackensack Meadowlands in New Jersey and at Jamaica Bay Wildlife Refuge, where they are also common winter residents.

Similar Species: Female Bufflehead (p. 41) has a white cheek patch like a winter male Ruddy Duck, but the Bufflehead has a smaller, thinner bill. All other waterfowl are generally larger and have shorter tails and relatively smaller heads.

Quick ID: small duck; broad bill; large head; tail is often cocked up. *Breeding male:* reddish-brown neck and body; black head and tail; white cheek; blue bill. *Non-breeding male:* dull brown overall; dark cap; white cheek. *Female:* like non-breeding male, but pale cheek has a dark stripe.
Size: 14–16 in.

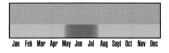

Jan Feb Mar Apr May Jun Jul Aug Sept Oct Nov Dec

Turkey Vulture
Cathartes aura

Soaring effortlessly above the landscape, Turkey Vultures ride rising thermals on warm afternoons, occasionally sailing over the Long Island area during migration, on their way to some unknown destination. They seldom need to flap their silver-lined wings, rocking gently from side to side as they carefully scan fields, roads, woodlands and shorelines for carcasses. Even at great distances, this bare-headed bird can be identified by the way it tends to hold its wings upward in a shallow V.

The Turkey Vulture feeds entirely on carrion, which it can sometimes detect by scent alone. The featherless head is an adaptation for staying clean and parasite-free while it digs around inside carcasses. This scavenger's well-known habit of regurgitating its rotting meal at intruders might be a defense mechanism—it allows Turkey Vultures to reduce their weight for a quicker take-off, and the smell helps young vultures repel would-be predators.

Similar Species: Hawks, eagles and Osprey (p. 46) all have large, feathered heads and tend to hold their wings flatter in flight, not in a shallow V.

Quick ID: larger than a hawk; sexes similar; all-black plumage; small, red head.
In flight: wings held in shallow V; silver-gray flight feathers; dark wing linings; rocks from side to side.
Size: 27–30 in.

Jan Feb Mar Apr May Jun Jul Aug Sept Oct Nov Dec

VULTURES, HAWKS & FALCONS 45

Osprey

Pandion haliaetus

In the New York City area, the Osprey is most often seen over large waterbodies during migration, primarily in April, September and October. Although a large population of Ospreys nests along the eastern tip of Long Island and in northeastern Suffolk County, the New York City area generally does not provide the nesting trees or platforms required to raise young. In our area the Osprey is also still recovering from the devastating effects of the heavy use of pesticides, such as DDT, and other forms of manmade pollution, which resulted in widespread reproductive failure in some raptor species only a few decades ago.

A hunting Osprey will survey the calm waters of a coastal bay from the air. Spotting a flash of silver underwater, the Osprey folds its great wings and dives toward the fish. An instant before striking the water, the bird thrusts its talons forward to grasp its slippery prey. The Osprey might completely disappear beneath the water to ensure a successful capture; then it reappears, slapping its wings on the surface as it returns to the air. Once it has regained flight, the Osprey shakes off the residual water and heads off toward its bulky stick nest, holding its prey facing forward to increase aerodynamic efficiency.

Similar Species: Bald Eagle is larger and never has the combination of clean white underparts and a white head with an eye streak. Other large raptors are seldom seen near water. Gulls don't have hooked bills and lack the combination of a brown back and white underparts.

Jan Feb Mar Apr May Jun Jul Aug Sept Oct Nov Dec

Quick ID: large hawk–sized; sexes similar; white underparts; dark elbow patches; white head; dark streak through eye. *In flight:* wings held in shallow M.
Size: 21–24 in.

Northern Harrier

Circus cyaneus

♂

This common marsh hawk can best be identified by its flight behavior: the Northern Harrier flies low over lush meadows and marshes, often retracing its path several times in the quest for prey. Watch the slow, lazy wingbeats of the Northern Harrier as this raptor skims the brambles and bulrushes with its belly. Unlike other hawks, which can find their prey only visually, the Northern Harrier stays close enough to the ground to listen for birds, voles and mice. When movement catches the Harrier's eyes or ears, it abandons its lazy ways to strike at its prey with channeled energy.

♀

Hunting harriers are abundant year-round residents in Jones Beach State Park, but they are generally common winter residents and uncommon breeders in the New York City area. They are most often observed over saltmarshes, grassy expanses and estuary shorelines, like those found at Jamaica Bay, Pelham Bay and John F. Kennedy International Airport. Troy Meadows in New Jersey has Northern Harriers in winter.

Similar Species: Short-eared Owl (p. 75) and Sharp-shinned (p. 48), Red-tailed (p. 50) and Cooper's hawks all lack the white rump. Rough-legged Hawk has a white rump, but it has a chunkier shape (shorter, broader wings and tail).

Quick ID: mid-sized hawk; white rump; long tail; long wings; owl-like face (seen only at close range). *Male:* grayish upperparts; whitish underparts; black wing tips. *Female:* brown overall. *Immature:* brown back; chestnut underparts.
Size: 20 in.

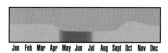

Jan Feb Mar Apr May Jun Jul Aug Sept Oct Nov Dec

-shinned Hawk

r striatus

If songbirds dream, the Sharp-shinned Hawk is sure to be the source of their nightmares. These raptors pursue small birds through forests, maneuvering around leaves and branches in the hope of striking down prey. Sharp-shinned Hawks prey on many birds, with small songbirds and the occasional woodpecker being the most numerous victims.

These small hawks are easy to find in wooded areas and in open skies as they pass through our area in April and again from mid-September to mid-October. During the winter months, at least a few of New York City's wooded neighborhoods have a resident 'Sharpie' eager to catch unwary finches, sparrows and starlings. Backyard feeders tend to concentrate these small birds, so they are attractive foraging areas for this small hawk. A sudden eruption of songbirds off the feeder and a few feathers floating on the wind are often the signs of a sudden, successful Sharp-shin attack.

Similar Species: Cooper's Hawk is larger, and its tail is rounded and has a wide terminal band. Merlin has pointed wings and rapid wingbeats, and it lacks the red chest barring of an adult Sharp-shinned Hawk.

Quick ID: pigeon-sized; sexes similar; short, round wings; long tail. *Adult:* blue-gray back; red barring on underparts; red eyes. *In flight:* flap-and-glide flier; barred tail is straight at end. *Immature:* brown overall; vertical, brown streaks on breast; yellow eyes.
Size: 12–14 in. (female larger).

Jan Feb Mar Apr May Jun Jul Aug Sept Oct Nov Dec

Broad-winged Hawk

Buteo platypterus

Sighting this mid-sized hawk is a hit-and-miss affair. Broad-winged Hawks are fairly secretive in their wooded breeding habitat, and many summers can pass without one being seen, even though they regularly breed in the wooded areas of northeastern Nassau County. However, a trip to Hook Mountain in Rockland County or another interior hawk-watching site from April 5 to 20 or from September 20 to October 10 can be a spectacular experience, and hundreds of migrating Broad-winged Hawks can often be seen in a single day! This peak of migration might occur on only three or four days, and the fall flights are best when driven by northwest winds.

Hawks' heavy wings are not designed for continual flapping flight, so these raptors seek out areas such as hills and mountains where they can soar on warm updrafts. The rising air currents help them gain altitude before they launch across a stretch of stagnant, heavy air.

Similar Species: Red-tailed Hawk (p. 50) has a solid red tail. Sharp-shinned Hawk (p. 48) has a long, narrow tail. Rough-legged Hawk is a winter visitor. Red-shouldered Hawk has red shoulders and narrow, white bands on its black tail.

Quick ID: smaller than a crow; sexes similar.
Adult: wide white bands on black, fan-like tail; russet barring on breast; rounded wings.
Immature: dark 'teardrops' on breast, black whisker streaks and indistinct barring on tail.
Size: 15–17 in.

Jan Feb Mar Apr May Jun Jul Aug Sept Oct Nov Dec

Although Sinatra wasn't singing about birds in his classic 'New York, New York' lyrics, the words hold true for the Red-tailed Hawk. As a species of raptor that has been able to nest successfully in Manhattan, this hawk has clearly shown that it can 'make it' just about anywhere. It is the most widespread and successful hawk in North America, breeding throughout most of the continent.

Its characteristic scream suggests that the Red-tail is a hawk best avoided. You would think other birds would treat this large raptor with more respect, but the Red-tailed Hawk is constantly being harassed by crows, jays and blackbirds.

Although they have nested in the city, Red-tailed Hawks are much more commonly encountered wherever highways pass through open country. It's hard not to spot a Red-tail in our area perched on a post or soaring lazily overhead, even when you are driving along at highway speeds.

Similar Species: Northern Harrier (p. 47) has a white rump and a long tail. Sharp-shinned Hawk (p. 48) and Cooper's Hawk are smaller and have long, slender tails. Broad-winged Hawk (p. 49) has a boldly banded tail. Rough-legged Hawk is a winter visitor with a wide, dark tail band and a black belly band. Red-shouldered Hawk has narrow, white bands on its black tail and red shoulders.

Jan Feb Mar Apr May Jun Jul Aug Sept Oct Nov Dec

Quick ID: large hawk; sexes similar; brick-red tail (adult only); brown head; variable, brown-speckled 'belt'; light flight feathers; dark wing lining and leading edge.
Size: 20–24 in.

American Kestrel

Falco sparverius

This small, noisy falcon is a loyal and dependable resident throughout much of the New York City area. It has adapted well to rural life, and it is commonly seen perched on power lines, watching for unwary grasshoppers, birds and rodents. When not perched, American Kestrels can often be seen hovering above potential prey. Kestrels are commonly encountered in fall along many highways, and they typically leave their power line perches as vehicles approach.

All falcons are skilled hunters, and they have a unique, tooth-like projection on their hooked bills that can quickly crush the necks of small prey. The American Kestrel's species name, *sparverius*, is Latin for 'pertaining to sparrows,' which are occasional prey items.

American Kestrels often build their nests in abandoned woodpecker cavities. Conservationists have discovered that kestrels will use nest boxes when natural cavities are unavailable, which should ensure that these active predators maintain their presence in our rural neighborhoods.

Similar Species: Sharp-shinned Hawk (p. 48) and Cooper's Hawk have short, rounder wings. Peregrine Falcon (p. 52) is much larger and lacks the contrasting ruddy and bluish colors. Merlin is larger, has a banded tail and lacks any russet coloration.

Quick ID: slightly smaller than a jay; long, pointed wings; long tail; two vertical, black stripes on sides of face; russet back; spotted breast; hooked bill. *In flight:* rapid wingbeats. *Male:* blue wings; colorful head. *Female:* russet wings.
Size: 9–11 in.

Jan Feb Mar Apr May Jun Jul Aug Sept Oct Nov Dec

rine Falcon
'regrinus

Whereas most tourists entering the metropolitan chasms of New York City gaze up in awe at skyscrapers, visiting birders' eyes glance skyward in the hope of seeing a Peregrine. It is one of the fastest animals in the world, reaching speeds of well over 100 m.p.h. Once a Peregrine has its prey singled out, even the fastest ducks, pigeons and shorebirds have little chance of escaping this effective predator.

New York State's Peregrines declined to near extinction because of pesticide residues in the environment. The banning of DDT and the implementation of an active recovery plan have recently allowed this endangered species to emerge from the brink of extinction, so that this magnificent bird can now be found breeding on skyscrapers and bridges around New York City. With our city acting as a stronghold for recovering Peregrines, New Yorkers can once again indulge in the delight and astonishment of watching these feathered rockets display their extraordinary hunting skills.

Similar Species: American Kestrel (p. 51) and Merlin are much smaller.

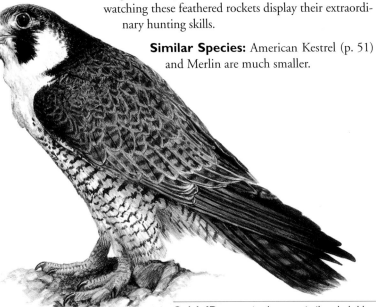

Quick ID: crow-sized; sexes similar; dark blue hood extending down cheek; steel blue upperparts; light underparts with dark speckles.
In flight: pointed wings; long tail. *Immature:* like adult except brown where adult is steel blue; more heavily streaked underparts.
Size: 15–20 in.

Jan Feb Mar Apr May Jun Jul Aug Sept Oct Nov Dec

Black-bellied Plover
Pluvialis squatarola

Black-bellied Plovers are regularly seen darting along sea beaches, grassy openings and plowed fields, foraging with a robin-like run-and-stop technique. Although they dress in plain grays for much of their New York City retreat, a few Black-bellied Plovers can be seen in their summer 'tuxedo' plumage in spring and early fall.

Although these plovers are most common in our area during spring and fall migration, a few birds can usually be observed poking around New York City–area beaches during the summer and winter months. Bring your binoculars with you on your next walk along Jones Beach or the North Shore of Nassau County—if you're lucky, you might see some Black-bellied Plovers scurrying along the sand ahead of you as they pluck the surface for food.

Similar Species: Willet is larger and slimmer and has a longer bill. Other shorebirds are not as plump or as gray.

non-breeding

Quick ID: larger than a robin; sexes similar; short, stout, black bill; relatively long, dark legs.
Non-breeding: slightly streaked, gray body.
In flight: black wing pits; white rump; white wing linings.
Size: 12 in.

Jan Feb Mar Apr May Jun Jul Aug Sept Oct Nov Dec

Piping Plover

Charadrius melodus

breeding

A master of illusion, the secretive Piping Plover is a rarely seen bird of the sandy ocean shore. Its pale body colors conceal it among the shoreline sand, while the dark bands across the forehead and breast look like stray pebbles or strips of washed-up vegetation that effectively disrupt its body form so that it no longer looks like a bird to potential predators. Even its four pale, pear-shaped eggs are speckled with dark colors to disguise them among the combination of sand, rocks, vegetation and scattered shell fragments that surround a typical nest.

Unfortunately, increased competition with people using the shoreline landscape continues to threaten the breeding success of this delightful but increasingly endangered bird. Learning to recognize its presence along the shores of New York City and the beaches of the Long Island coast, and helping to promote its needs for privacy, might ensure that it remains a treasured part of the New York City area for years to come.

Similar Species: Semipalmated Plover has a dark back and dark facial bands connecting the eyes to the bill.

Quick ID: smaller than a robin; sexes similar; white underparts; pale gray back; black forehead band connecting eyes; black collar band often connects across breast; orange legs; orange bill tipped with black. *In flight:* white rump.
Size: 7¼ in.

Jan Feb Mar Apr May Jun Jul Aug Sept Oct Nov Dec

Killdeer

Charadrius vociferus

The Killdeer is the most widespread 'shorebird' in the New York City area. It nests on gravelly shorelines, utility rights-of-way, lawns, pastures and occasionally on gravel roofs and parking lots within the city, well away from shore. Its name is a paraphrase of its distinctive, loud call: *kill-dee kill-dee kill-deer!*

The Killdeer's response to predators relies on deception and good acting skills. To divert a predator's attention away from a nest or a brood of young, an adult Killdeer (like many shorebirds) will flop around to feign an injury (usually a broken wing). Once the Killdeer has the attention of the fox, crow, gull or human, it leads the predator away from the vulnerable nest. After it reaches a safe distance, the adult Killdeer is suddenly 'healed' and flies off, leaving the predator without a meal.

Similar Species: Semipalmated Plover has only one chest band, is smaller and is found mostly on mudflats.

Quick ID: robin-sized; sexes similar; two black bands across breast; brown back; russet rump; long legs; white underparts.
Size: 9–11 in.

Jan Feb Mar Apr May Jun Jul Aug Sept Oct Nov Dec

Greater Yellowlegs

Tringa melanoleuca

On a spring walk along the shores of New York City and Long Island, you can see quite a few different sandpipers. The Greater Yellowlegs, one of our largest and most noticeable shorebirds, prefers shallow pools where it can peck for small invertebrates, but it won't hesitate to venture belly-deep into the water to pursue prey. Occasionally, a yellowlegs can be seen hopping along on one leg, with the other one tucked up in the body feathers to reduce heat loss.

non-breeding

Many birders enjoy the challenge of distinguishing the Greater Yellowlegs from the Lesser Yellowlegs. The Greater, which is slightly more common in the New York City area (but don't let that bias your identification), has a relatively longer, heavier bill. Its bill is also slightly upturned—so slightly, however, that you notice it one moment and not the next. Generally, the Lesser's call is *tew tew*, and the Greater's is *tew tew tew*. Cocky birders will name them at a glance, but more experienced birders will tell you that many of these people are bluffing—much of the time you can only write 'unidentified yellowlegs' in your field notes.

Similar Species: Sanderling (p. 58), Dunlin (p. 61) and Western Sandpiper are all much smaller and have dark legs. Lesser Yellowlegs is smaller and has a shorter bill. Willet has bluish legs and a thicker, straighter bill.

Jan Feb Mar Apr May Jun Jul Aug Sept Oct Nov Dec

Quick ID: pigeon-sized; sexes similar; long, bright yellow legs; finely streaked, gray body; bill is longer than head width.
Size: 13–15 in.

Ruddy Turnstone

Arenaria interpres

non-breeding

During migration, Ruddy Turnstones stop on the sandy and pebbly beaches that are found in many areas along our shores. The beaches and mudflats at Jamaica Bay, Great Kills Park and Jones Beach are terrific places to see large flocks of turnstones mixed in with other species of shorebirds.

Ruddy Turnstones do much of their foraging by probing in the wet sand and between small rocks for amphipods and other small invertebrates that live buried along the shoreline, but they have gained fame for an unusual feeding technique. As its name implies, a turnstone often flips over small rocks and ocean debris with its bill to expose hidden invertebrates. The turnstone's bill is short, stubby and slightly upturned—ideal for this foraging style.

Similar Species: Dunlin (p. 61) has a downcurved bill and lacks the bold patterning.

Quick ID: robin-sized; sexes similar (female is slightly paler); white belly; black bib; stout, slightly upturned bill; orange-red legs. *Breeding:* ruddy upperparts; white face; black collar; gray crown. *Non-breeding:* dark brownish upperparts and face.
Size: 9–10 in.

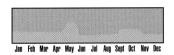

Jan Feb Mar Apr May Jun Jul Aug Sept Oct Nov Dec

Sanderling

Calidris alba

A spring or fall stroll at Jones Beach, Jamaica Bay or Great Kills Park is often punctuated by the sight of these tiny runners, which appear to enjoy nothing more than playing in the surf. Sanderlings are characteristically seen chasing and retreating from the rolling waves, never getting caught in the charging water. Only the Sanderling commonly forages in this manner, plucking at the exposed invertebrates stirred up by the wave action. When there are no waves to chase along calm shorelines, Sanderlings unenthusiastically probe into wet soil in much the same fashion as many other sandpipers.

This sandpiper is one of the world's most widespread birds. It breeds across the Arctic in Alaska, Canada and Russia, and it spends winter running up and down sandy shorelines in North America, South America, Asia, Africa and Australia. Every year, hundreds of these birds choose to brave the winter along the wave-swept beaches of New York City and Long Island.

Similar Species: Least Sandpiper (p. 60) is smaller and browner. Dunlin (p. 61) is darker gray and has a downcurved bill.

non-breeding

Quick ID: smaller than a robin; sexes similar; straight, black bill; dark legs. *Breeding:* rusty head and breast. *Non-breeding:* white underparts; grayish-white upperparts; black shoulder patch (sometimes concealed).
Size: 7 1/2–8 1/2 in.

Jan Feb Mar Apr May Jun Jul Aug Sept Oct Nov Dec

Semipalmated Sandpiper

Calidris pusilla

New York City birders are privileged to feast on the great migrations of these spectacular 'wind birds.' From late April to June, and again from July into September, New York City and Long Island shorelines are visited by synchronized flocks of Semipalmated Sandpipers. Between mass flights of astounding synchrony, they peck and probe in mechanized fury, replenishing their body fat for the remainder of their long trip. Semipalmated Sandpipers migrate almost the entire length of the Americas, and they require that their migratory pit stops provide ample food resources.

Although the New York City area does not host the abundance of Semis found along the windswept shores of eastern Long Island, our wetlands and beaches are just as vital to the survival of smaller groups of these feathered delights. Jones Beach State Park is a particularly good place to look for Semipalmated Sandpipers mixed among flocks of other shorebirds.

'Semipalmated' refers to the slight webbing between this bird's front toes. The scientific name *pusilla* is Latin for 'petty' or 'small.'

Similar Species: Least Sandpiper (p. 60) has pale legs. Dunlin (p. 61) has a downcurved bill. Western Sandpiper has a longer, slightly downcurved bill. White-rumped Sandpiper has an all-white rump and wings that extend beyond the tail.

non-breeding

Quick ID: smaller than a robin; sexes similar; short, straight, all-dark bill; dark legs.
Breeding: mottled upperparts; rufous ear patch; faint streaks on upper breast and flanks.
Non-breeding: gray-brown upperparts; white underparts; faint, white eyebrow.
In flight: narrow, white wing stripe; white rump split by black line.
Size: 5¹/₂–7 in.

Jan Feb Mar Apr May Jun Jul Aug Sept Oct Nov Dec

Least Sandpiper
Calidris minutilla

The Least Sandpiper is the smallest of our shorebirds, but its size is not a deterrent to its migratory feats. Like most other 'peeps'—a term used to group the sometimes difficult to identify, small *Calidris* sandpipers—the Least Sandpipers passing through New York City migrate to the Arctic to breed.

Groups of these tiny birds can be seen on mudflats and beaches throughout our area. Exploring the North Shore of Nassau County should be productive in early May and throughout September in your search for Least Sandpipers. Their plumage matches perfectly with their preferred habitat, and it is usually their rapid movements that reveal these diminutive sprinters. Least Sandpipers tenaciously peck the moist substrate with their dexterous bills, eating mosquitoes, beach fleas, amphipods and other aquatic invertebrates.

Similar Species: Pectoral Sandpiper is larger and has a well-defined border on the breast. Other 'peeps' tend to have dark legs and are generally larger.

non-breeding

Quick ID: sparrow-sized; sexes similar.
Adult: black bill; yellow legs; dark, mottled back; buff-brown breast, head and nape; light breast streaking. *Immature:* like adult, but with faintly streaked breast.
Size: 5–6 in.

Jan Feb Mar Apr May Jun Jul Aug Sept Oct Nov Dec

Dunlin

Calidris alpina

Outside the breeding season, Dunlins are communal creatures that form swirling clouds of hundreds of individuals flying wing tip to wing tip, all changing course simultaneously, as if one entity. These hypnotic flights, which flash alternating shades of white and dark, are occasionally seen as Dunlins migrate along New York City's coastline. These tight flocks are generally more exclusive than many other shorebird troupes: few species mix with groups of Dunlins. Watch for their peak migration along Great Kills Park and Jones Beach in late May and throughout October.

The Dunlin, like many other shorebirds, nests on the Arctic tundra and winters on the coasts of North America, Europe and Asia. This bird was originally called the 'Dunling' (meaning 'a small brown bird'), but for unknown reasons the 'g' was later dropped.

Similar Species: Least Sandpiper (p. 60) is smaller. Sanderling (p. 58) is paler and is usually seen running in the surf. Purple Sandpiper has orange-yellow legs and a more mottled appearance than a winter Dunlin.

non-breeding

Quick ID: smaller than a robin; sexes similar; slightly downcurved bill; dark legs. *Breeding:* black belly; streaked underparts; rusty back. *Non-breeding:* pale gray underparts; grayish-brown upperparts.
Size: 8–9 in.

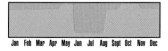

Jan Feb Mar Apr May Jun Jul Aug Sept Oct Nov Dec

Short-billed Dowitcher

Limnodromus griseus

non-breeding

When the fall tides are at their highest, shorebirds concentrate in large numbers along mudflats, marshes and estuaries in the Long Island area. High tides force dowitchers and other migrating shorebirds to high, dry ground, often packing them together in large numbers. Dowitchers tend to be stockier than most shorebirds, and they avoid deeper water. The sewing machine–like rhythms that dowitchers perform while foraging deeply into the mudflats is helpful for field identification. Look for the Short-billed Dowitcher at Jones Beach from May to the end of July.

This bird can only be called 'short-billed' in comparison to its long-billed relative. Unfortunately, separating the two Long Island dowitcher species is one of the most difficult tasks any birder can attempt, so most people are perfectly content to simply call them 'dowitchers.'

Similar Species: Long-billed Dowitcher is darker overall; in non-breeding plumage it has an unmarked, dark gray breast; and in breeding plumage it has black spots on the breast and maroon flanks. Common Snipe has longer legs, heavily barred upperparts and different foraging techniques.

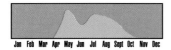

Jan Feb Mar Apr May Jun Jul Aug Sept Oct Nov Dec

Quick ID: larger than a robin; sexes similar; very long, straight, dark bill; very stocky body; short neck. *Breeding:* reddish underparts; lightly barred flanks; dark, mottled upperparts; dark eye line; light eyebrow; dark yellow legs; white rump. *Non-breeding:* gray overall; white belly.
Size: 11–12¹/₂ in. (female larger).

Laughing Gull

Larus atricilla

breeding

Imagine how fun it would be to fly over New York City and watch the frantic urban antics of the people below. Maybe that is why the well-named Laughing Gull hurls its endless laugh across the city landscape. Of course, its raucous call might also be perceived as a triumphant expression of joy from overcoming hardship and near extermination. By the late 1800s, the high commercial demand for egg collections and feathers for women's hats nearly wiped out the breeding population of Laughing Gulls in the New York City area. Only in recent decades has this resolute gull been allowed to recover and return to breed each summer in the saltmarshes of Jamaica Bay.

Similar Species: Bonaparte's Gull is smaller, has a black bill and orange feet and is more common in winter, when its head is mostly white with a black ear spot. Little Gull is smaller, and both it and the Black-headed Gull are seen in winter, when each has a white head with a black ear spot.

Quick ID: small gull; sexes similar; black head; red bill; black feet; incomplete, white eye ring; white neck and underparts; dark gray back; black-tipped wings.
Size: 16½ in.

Jan Feb Mar Apr May Jun Jul Aug Sept Oct Nov Dec

Ring-billed Gull

Larus delawarensis

The Ring-billed Gull likes the Big Apple well enough to set up shop here on a permanent, year-round basis even though (unlike several other gull species) it doesn't breed in our area. This mid-sized gull can usually be distinguished from other gulls by its combination of a gray back, yellow legs and the black ring around both the upper and lower mandible, near the tip of the otherwise yellow bill.

Once the frantic nesting season is over, both adult and immature Ring-bills can be encountered throughout the New York City and Long Island region. Over the fall and winter months, they associate with other flocks of gulls in city parks, in shopping center parking lots, near fastfood restaurants and on local lakes and ponds. These birds are infamous for their raucous food-scavenging and windshield-fouling exploits, making New York City that much wilder a place in which to live.

Similar Species: Adult Herring Gull (p. 65) and Great Black-backed Gull (p. 66) lack the black bill ring. Immature gulls of other species can have black on the tip of the bill, but none show this feature with a yellow bill and feet.

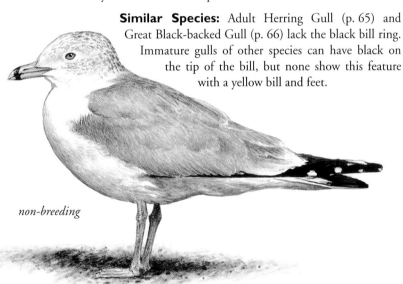

non-breeding

Quick ID: mid-sized gull; sexes similar; black ring near bill tip; yellow bill and legs; gray wings and back; light eyes; black wing tips; small white spots on black primaries; white underparts. *Non-breeding*: white head and nape washed with brown. *1st winter*: mottled grayish brown; gray back; blackish-brown primaries; black tail band. **Size:** 18–20 in.

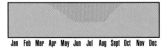

Jan Feb Mar Apr May Jun Jul Aug Sept Oct Nov Dec

Herring Gull

Larus argentatus

Many gulls come and go in New York City, but the Herring Gull is a year-round resident, particularly along the coast. Although this familiar bird is commonly referred to as a 'seagull,' it does not rightfully deserve that moniker, because several other gulls are more closely tied to salt water. Large flocks of this gull can be found in bays, lakes, garbage dumps, shorelines, city parks and agricultural fields. Herring Gulls are so widely distributed that they are sure to be sighted on just about any birding trip taken around New York City or Long Island.

Like other large gulls, the Herring Gull takes many years to achieve adult plumage. It starts out dark brown, and each successive plumage more closely resembles that of the adult. Although it is often overlooked by even the most curious naturalist, the Herring Gull is an engineering marvel. Agile on land, an effortless flier, wonderfully adaptive and with a stomach for anything digestible, the Herring Gull is perhaps the most widely distributed gull in North America.

Similar Species: Ring-billed Gull (p. 64) has yellow legs and a black band around the tip of the bill. Glaucous Gull and Iceland Gull have lighter backs and wings and lack the black wing tips.

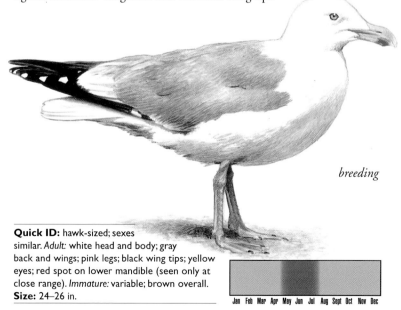

breeding

Quick ID: hawk-sized; sexes similar. *Adult:* white head and body; gray back and wings; pink legs; black wing tips; yellow eyes; red spot on lower mandible (seen only at close range). *Immature:* variable; brown overall.
Size: 24–26 in.

Jan Feb Mar Apr May Jun Jul Aug Sept Oct Nov Dec

Great Black-backed Gull

Larus marinus

Surrounded by productive sources of fresh and salt water, and home to a few million food waste–generating humans, the New York City area is gull paradise. This is particularly true for North America's largest gull, the aggressive and dominating Great Black-backed Gull. A year-round resident, this bird is easily identified among other gulls of our city by its black mantle and commanding proportions.

This bird nests in large colonies each summer, usually near or among a nesting colony of Herring Gulls. Successful breeding colonies are usually situated on islands close to a reliable source of food and isolated from the threat of hungry mammals, such as rats, skunks, weasels and foxes. Just as Great Black-backs avoid predatory mammals, many species of tern and other seabirds avoid the aggressive instincts of this formidable bird.

Similar Species: Herring Gull (p. 65) and Ring-billed Gull (p. 64) have light gray upperparts, and the Ring-bill has yellow legs and a black band around the tip of its bill. Lesser Black-backed Gull has a dark gray mantle, black wing tips and yellow legs.

breeding

Jan Feb Mar Apr May Jun Jul Aug Sept Oct Nov Dec

Quick ID: very large gull; sexes similar; white head, neck and underparts, except for gray underside of wings; black upperparts; pale pink legs; pale eyes; large yellow bill with red spot on lower mandible.
Size: 29–31 in.

Common Tern
Sterna hirundo

The Common Tern generally goes unnoticed until a splash draws attention to its headfirst dives into water. Once it has firmly seized a small fish in its black-tipped bill, the tern bounces back into the air and continues its leisurely flight. Common Terns are easily observed from May to September, working the shores of Rockaway Peninsula and Atlantic Beach. Although some terns continue northward during spring migration, many remain in our area to nest.

Although terns and gulls share many of the same physical characteristics, there are features that clearly separate the two groups. Terns seldom rest on the water, and they rarely soar in flight, whereas gulls never plunge-dive into the water after fish. Also, terns have very short necks, pointed wings and long, forked tails, and they tend to look toward the ground during flight. Both gulls and terns tend to nest in similar regions, but this may be more convenient for the gulls, because they routinely prey on the smaller terns and their chicks.

Similar Species: Least Tern (p. 68) has a white forehead. Gull-billed Tern has a black bill and legs. Roseate Tern only has red at the base of the bill and has a much longer forked tail. Caspian Tern has a large, red bill and is gull-sized. Forster's Tern has a grayer tail and frosted wing tips.

breeding

Quick ID: larger than a pigeon; sexes similar; black cap; orange bill tipped with black; gray back and wings; white throat and belly. *In flight:* pointed wings; forked tail; often hovers.
Size: 14–16 in.

Jan Feb Mar Apr May Jun Jul Aug Sept Oct Nov Dec

Least Tern

Sterna antillarum

breeding

On hot, sunny, summer weekends, one can appreciate the Least Tern's dilemma. Out-of-state tourists and New Yorkers flock to crowded beaches, where finding a place to lay down your towel can be difficult. Although people visit Long Island beaches for pleasure, Least Terns are there out of necessity—they nest exclusively on open, sandy beaches. This tern's nest is a simple, hollow scrape in the sand. Provided that the nest is not raided by a predator or inadvertently destroyed by beach-goers, the one to three young will hatch in 20 to 25 days.

This threatened species is now restricted to breeding in a few scattered, protected areas, which are usually fenced off to protect them from humans. The courtship rituals of North America's smallest tern are quite elaborate, and they include pre-nuptial flights and feeding interactions. Terns are among the few animals (including humans) that present gifts to potential mates. With increased awareness, it is possible that both humans and species like the Least Tern can share the rich assets of New York's precious coastal beaches.

Similar Species: Common (p. 67), Forster's and Caspian terns are much larger, lack the white forehead and have red or orange bills.

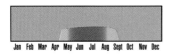

Jan Feb Mar Apr May Jun Jul Aug Sept Oct Nov Dec

Quick ID: robin-sized; sexes similar; black cap; white forehead; yellow bill with a black tip. *In flight:* long, tapered wings with black outer edges.
Size: 9–10 in.

Black Skimmer

Rynchops niger

breeding

There are many odd sights in New York City, but for the first-time birdwatcher, the sight of a Black Skimmer must rank near the top of the list. This bird appears completely out of proportion: its lower mandible extends well beyond its upper one. Such a cumbersome bill looks wonderfully ridiculous, but when the skimmer's foraging strategy is known, the structure is justified.

With slow, deliberate wingbeats, the Black Skimmer skims over calm waters. It flies so low that if it arches its neck down and holds its bill open, the lower mandible cuts through the water's surface. With the mandible now slicing through the water, small fish and invertebrates near the surface are seized with a lightning reflex.

For many years, New Yorkers had no opportunity to observe this great adaptation. It wasn't until the 1920s that New Yorkers began seeing the Black Skimmer on a regular basis, followed with breeding evidence in 1934. Now, birders from Breezy Point to Montauk can be treated routinely to the unusual sights of Black Skimmers.

Similar Species: Caspian Tern has lighter upperparts and a shorter lower mandible.

Quick ID: small gull–sized; sexes similar; red bill, tipped with black; lower mandible longer than upper; dark upperparts; light underparts; red legs.
Size: 16–20 in.

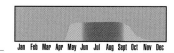

Jan Feb Mar Apr May Jun Jul Aug Sept Oct Nov Dec

Rock Dove
Columba livia

The ubiquitous urban Rock Dove, widely known as the 'Pigeon,' has taken advantage of humans for food and shelter. This Eurasian native breeds and roosts on buildings, ledges and bridges, and it feeds primarily on waste grain and human handouts. It was first brought to North America in 1606 as a food source, but it quickly became a popular pet. Rock Doves soon dispersed from the East Coast to colonize the entire continent, with many birds returning to their ancestral habits of nesting on cliffs and surviving on wild seeds and berries.

Rock Doves might appear strained when they walk—their heads move back and forth with every step—but few birds are as agile in flight or as abundant in urban and industrial areas. Although no other bird varies as much in coloration, all Rock Doves, whether white, red, blue or mixed-pigment, will clap their wings above and below their bodies upon take-off.

Similar Species: Mourning Dove (p. 71) is the same length as the Rock Dove, but it is slender and has a long, tapering tail and olive-brown plumage.

Jan Feb Mar Apr May Jun Jul Aug Sept Oct Nov Dec

Quick ID: mid-sized pigeon; sexes similar; variable color (iridescent blue-gray, black, red or white); white rump (usually); orange feet; bill is fleshy at base.
Size: 13–14 in.

Mourning Dove

Zenaida macroura

As a Mourning Dove bursts into flight, its wings 'clap' above and below its body for the first few wingbeats. The Mourning Dove is a swift, direct flier, and its wings can be heard whistling through the air. When it is not in flight, the Mourning Dove's peaceful, *coooah-coooo-cooooo-coooo* call can be heard filtering through open woodlands. These year-round residents roost inconspicuously in trees, but their soft cooing often betrays their presence.

The Mourning Dove feeds primarily on the ground in open areas, picking up seeds and the odd piece of grit to help grind down hard seed coatings. It builds a flat, loose stick nest that rests flimsily on branches and trunks. Mourning Doves are attentive parents, and, like other members of the pigeon family, they feed 'milk' to their young. It isn't true milk—birds don't have mammary glands—but a fluid produced by glands in the bird's crop. The chicks insert their bills down the adult's throat to drink the rich, thick liquid meal.

Similar Species: Rock Dove (p. 70) has a white rump, is stockier and has a shorter tail.

Quick ID: jay-sized; sexes similar; gray-brown plumage; long, white-trimmed, tapering tail; sleek body; dark, shiny patch below ear; orange feet; dark bill; buff-colored underparts.
Size: 11–13 in.

Jan Feb Mar Apr May Jun Jul Aug Sept Oct Nov Dec

Yellow-billed Cuckoo

Coccyzus americanus

From deep within the dark, dense marsh-side thickets escapes a jungle-like call: *ku-ku-ku-ku-ka-ka-kowk-kowk-kowk*. This strange, mysterious cry might be the only evidence of your meeting with one of New York City's elusive and highly secretive cuckoos. Both Yellow-billed and Black-billed cuckoos elude the most patient of observers, relying on secrecy to survive the pressures of urban chaos.

Unlike most bird species, which find hairy caterpillars to be unpalatable, cuckoos eat large numbers of them during caterpillar population outbreaks. Although cuckoos eat a variety of foods, their populations often rise and fall as a result of increases and decreases in the populations of these caterpillars. Keep your eyes and ears peeled for signs of these intriguing birds during your next visit to Staten Island or the North Shore of Nassau County.

Similar Species: Black-billed Cuckoo has a red eye ring and lacks the yellow on the bill and the rufous tinge on primaries, and its call is a repeated *cu-cu-cu* or *cu-cu-cu-cu*.

Jan Feb Mar Apr May Jun Jul Aug Sept Oct Nov Dec

Quick ID: larger than a robin; sexes similar; grayish-brown upperparts; white underparts; primary feathers tinged with rufous; down-curved bill with yellow lower mandible; long tail.
Size: 11–12 in.

Eastern Screech-Owl

Otus asio

Despite its small size, the Eastern Screech-Owl is a versatile hunter. It has a varied diet that ranges from insects, earthworms and fish to birds larger than itself. Silent and reclusive by day, screech-owls hunt at night. Strolling through the woodland parks of Staten Island or the North Shore Wildlife Sanctuary during an early spring evening, a person with a keen ear might hear the distinctive, whistled, quavering voice of the Eastern Screech-Owl.

Most owls' senses are refined for darkness and their bodies for silence. Their large, forward-facing eyes have many times more light-gathering sensors than do ours, and the wings of nocturnal owls are edged with frayed feathers for silent flight. Their ears, which occupy a large part of the sides of their heads, are asymmetrical (one is higher than the other), which enables these birds to pinpoint sounds more easily. Given these adaptations, it is no surprise that owls have successfully invaded nearly all of the world's major ecosystems.

gray phase

Similar Species: Northern Saw-whet Owl has a dark facial disc and no ear tufts.

Quick ID: robin-sized; sexes similar; short, widely spaced ear tufts; heavy vertical streaking and bars on breast; yellow eyes; dark bill; two color phases (red and gray).
Size: 8–9 in. (female slightly larger).

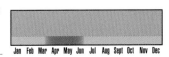

Jan Feb Mar Apr May Jun Jul Aug Sept Oct Nov Dec

Great Horned Owl
Bubo virginianus

The Great Horned Owl is the most widely distributed owl in North America, and it is among the most formidable of predators. It uses specialized hearing, powerful talons and human-sized eyes during nocturnal hunts for mice, rabbits, birds, amphibians and occasionally fish. It has a poorly developed sense of smell, however, and it frequently preys on skunks—worn-out and discarded Great Horned Owl feathers are often identifiable by a simple sniff.

The deep, resonant hooting of the Great Horned Owl is easily imitated, often leading to interesting exchanges between bird and birder. The call's deep tone is not as distinctive as its pace, which closely follows the rhythm of *eat my food, I'll-eat yooou*. Like most owls, Great Horned Owls are quite capable of seeing and hunting during daylight hours, but they tend to hunt under lower light conditions when their prey seem to be more active and available to be snatched.

Similar Species: Eastern Screech-Owl (p. 73) is much smaller and has vertical breast streaking. Long-eared Owl has a slimmer body and vertical streaks on its breast, and its ear tufts are very close together. Barn Owl has a white face and lacks ear tufts.

Quick ID: large hawk–sized; sexes similar; large, widely spaced ear tufts; fine, horizontal barring on breast; dark brown plumage; white throat.
Size: 18–25 in.

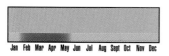

Jan Feb Mar Apr May Jun Jul Aug Sept Oct Nov Dec

Short-eared Owl

Asio flammeus

The Short-eared Owl's deep, lazy flapping makes it look more like a giant moth than like a bird. Near dawn and dusk, this predator of voles and mice is seen perched on fenceposts or flying over grassy meadows and marshes, searching for prey. This owl's name is quite misleading, because its 'ears' (actually nothing more than feather tufts) are so short that they're rarely seen.

The Short-eared Owl is quickly losing nesting and foraging habitat in New York City and Long Island. As fields and meadows are developed, the Short-eared Owl is increasingly pushed out of our area. It still breeds around Jamaica Bay and Jones Beach, where it is regularly seen low over golden fields, and it can be found at Troy Meadows in New Jersey in winter.

Similar Species: Female and immature Northern Harriers (p. 47) have a white rump and a small head. Barn Owl has unstreaked underparts and a white face. Long-eared Owl has distinctive ear tufts when perched.

Quick ID: crow-sized; sexes similar; large, round head; yellow eyes encircled by black; vertical streaks on chest, belly and back; long wings; black wrist patches; flight is distinctive.
Size: 13–17 in.

Jan Feb Mar Apr May Jun Jul Aug Sept Oct Nov Dec

Common Nighthawk

Chordeiles minor

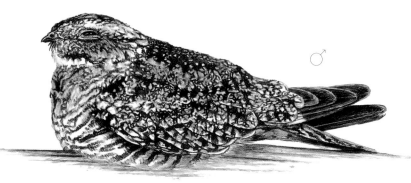

The Common Nighthawk has two distinct personalities: mild-mannered by day, it rests on the ground or on a horizontal tree branch, its color and shape blending perfectly into the texture of the bark; at dusk, it takes on a new form as a dazzling and erratic flier, catching insects in flight. You are most likely to see this bird from late May to the end of August during its twilight hunting forays.

To many people, the sounds of nighthawks are the sounds of summer evenings, and the recent declines in their numbers have left many naturalists longing for their previously common calls. The fascinating courtship of Common Nighthawks occurs over forest openings, beaches and urban areas. The nighthawks repeatedly call out with a loud, nasal *peeent* as they circle high overhead; then they dive suddenly toward the ground and create a hollow *vroom* by thrusting their wings forward at the last possible moment, pulling out of the dive.

Similar Species: Whip-poor-will and Chuck-will's-widow have rounded tails and wings and lack the white wrist bands.

Quick ID: robin-sized; sexes similar; cryptic, light to dark brown plumage; pale throat.
In flight: long, pointed wings; white wrist bands; shallowly forked tail; flight is erratic.
Size: 9–10 in.

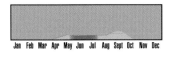

Jan Feb Mar Apr May Jun Jul Aug Sept Oct Nov Dec

Belted Kingfisher

Ceryle alcyon

As the name suggests, kingfishers primarily prey on fish, which they catch with precise, headfirst dives. A dead branch extending over water will often serve as a perch from which a Belted Kingfisher can survey the fish below.

The Belted Kingfisher builds its nest near the end of a long tunnel excavated a few feet into a sandy or dirt bank. A rattling call—similar to a teacup shaking on a saucer—along with blue-gray coloration and a large crest are the distinctive features of the Belted Kingfisher. In most birds the males are more colorful, but female kingfishers are distinguished from males by the presence of a second, rust-colored band across the belly.

Although there are many species of kingfishers in the world, the Belted Kingfisher is the only member of its family across most of the United States. Where open water is found in the New York City area, Belted Kingfishers can often be encountered crashing into calm waters in search of fish.

Similar Species: Blue Jay (p. 89) has a smaller crest, longer tail and smaller bill.

Quick ID: pigeon-sized; blue-gray back, wings and head; shaggy crest; heavy bill. *Male:* single, blue breast band. *Female:* blue breast band and rust-colored 'belt.'
Size: 12–14 in.

Jan Feb Mar Apr May Jun Jul Aug Sept Oct Nov Dec

Red-bellied Woodpecker

Melanerpes carolinus

♂

♀

An unexpected vocal *churr,*
emanating from deciduous
woodlands and parks throughout our area, is often the first
clue that the oddly named
Red-bellied Woodpecker is about. A
generally rare but locally common resident of
our area, this woodpecker mysteriously acquired
a name that reflects a very subtle field mark.
Because the 'Red-headed' moniker is granted to a more deserving woodpecker, perhaps a better name for this bird would have been the 'Zebra-
backed Woodpecker.'

Although it is continually threatened by bullying starlings, recent increases in the number of birdfeeders around the city have helped this
woodpecker survive our winters. Many New York City birdwatchers
fondly remember the chilly winter day when this striking bird first visited
their sunflower seed feeder. Although the seed source may be completely
reliable throughout the cold months, Red-bellied Woodpeckers take no
chances, and hoard the food, filling tree cavities, gaps in shingles, and
other small spaces with insurance seeds.

Similar Species: Northern Flicker (p. 80) has black-spotted underparts, yellow wing and tail linings and black-and-brown instead of black-
and-white barring on the back. Red-headed Woodpecker has a solid red
head and a solid black upper back.

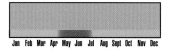

Jan Feb Mar Apr May Jun Jul Aug Sept Oct Nov Dec

Quick ID: robin-sized; black-and-white barring
on back; red crown and nape; plain gray face
and underparts; very faint red belly; white rump.
Male: red forehead. *Female:* gray forehead.
Size: 9–10 in.

Downy Woodpecker

Picoides pubescens

Soft taps carry through the trees of Central Park, sounding out the activities of a Downy Woodpecker. It methodically searches for hidden invertebrates by chipping off dead bark and probing into crevices. This woodpecker's small bill is amazingly effective at removing tiny slabs of bark, which rain down to the forest floor. The Downy Woodpecker is a systematic forager, and because of its small bill, it can find food where larger-billed woodpeckers cannot reach. When all the nooks of a tree have been probed, the Downy looks about and gives a chipper note before moving on to explore neighboring trees.

This black-and-white bird is the smallest North American woodpecker, and it is common in most woodlots, city parks and neighborhoods with a good population of trees. Backyard feeders filled with suet are especially attractive to this friendly and trusting delight. The male is readily distinguished from the female by a small patch of red feathers on the back of his head.

Similar Species: Hairy Woodpecker is larger and has a longer bill and clean white outer tail feathers.

Quick ID: large sparrow–sized; black-and-white wings and back; unmarked, white underparts; short, stubby bill; white outer tail feathers are spotted black. *Male:* red patch on back of head. *Female:* no red patch.
Size: 6–7 in.

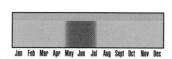

Jan Feb Mar Apr May Jun Jul Aug Sept Oct Nov Dec

Northern Flicker

Colaptes auratus

Walkers strolling through any of our larger parks might be surprised by a woodpecker flushing from the ground before them. As the Northern Flicker beats a hasty retreat, it reveals an unmistakable white rump and yellow wing linings. It is the least arboreal of our woodpeckers, and it spends much of its time feeding on the ground. Only when the Northern Flicker is around its nest cavity in a tree does it truly behave like other woodpeckers: clinging, rattling and drumming.

The Northern Flicker can be seen year-round in the wilder parts of the city, and it is especially abundant during October migration. It occasionally visits backyard feeders, but it is certainly less common through our winters. The Northern Flicker, like some other birds, has the peculiar, but ingenious, habit of squashing ants and then preening itself with the remains. Ants contain concentrations of formic acid, which is believed to kill small parasites living on the flicker's skin and in its feathers.

Similar Species: Red-bellied Woodpecker (p. 76) has a red crown and black-and-white bars on its back.

Quick ID: jay-sized; brown-barred back; spotted underparts; black bib; white rump; long bill; yellow wing and tail linings; gray crown; red nape. *Male:* black mustache. *Female:* no mustache.
Size: 11–14 in.

Jan Feb Mar Apr May Jun Jul Aug Sept Oct Nov Dec

Ruby-throated Hummingbird
Archilochus colubris

You are fortunate if you manage to get a prolonged look at a Ruby-throated Hummingbird, the only eastern hummingbird. Most meetings are over before they begin—a loud hum draws your attention to a small object zinging about, but it quickly disappears through the trees. Its identity is realized often only after the bird has disappeared.

Fortunately, Ruby-throated Hummingbirds are easily attracted to feeders of sweetened water (one part white sugar to four parts water). The male's iridescent ruby throat and emerald back play with the sunlight in ever-switching colors. The Ruby-throated Hummingbird's gentle appearance is misleading, however, and these fiercely aggressive birds will chase intruders away in spirited defense of a food source or prospective mates.

Hummingbirds are among the few birds able to fly vertically and in reverse. They can even flip backward and briefly fly upside-down to escape approaching danger. Amazingly, the wings of a hummingbird beat up to 80 times a second, and its heart can beat up to 1200 times a minute—compare that to our feeble 60- to 120-beat-per-minute hearts!

Similar Species: No birds, but possibly a hawkmoth.

Quick ID: our smallest bird; iridescent green back; long, thin, dark bill. *Male:* iridescent ruby throat.
Size: 4 in.

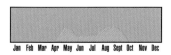

Jan Feb Mar Apr May Jun Jul Aug Sept Oct Nov Dec

Willow Flycatcher

Empidonax traillii

From its swaying willow perch, the Willow Flycatcher sings its chipper *fitz-bew* while surveying its chosen territory. Look for this feisty sprite in brushy and marshy lowland areas in and around New York City. Fresh Kills Park, Jamaica Bay and the North Shore Wildlife Sanctuary are all good places to observe it.

New York City, Long Island and northeastern New Jersey are exceptionally rich areas for flycatchers—the Willow, Alder, Acadian, Yellow-bellied and Least flycatchers can all be seen here during migration. Empidonax flycatchers (named after their genus) occur throughout North America, and they are famous in birdwatching circles for being hard to identify. Their plumages have slight variations that are obvious only under ideal conditions, but they can best be distinguished from each other by voice and habitat.

Similar Species: Least, Alder, Acadian and Yellow-bellied flycatchers all have distinctive, simple calls: Least sings *che-bek, che-bek, che-bek*; Alder sings a spunky *free-beer*; Acadian gives a forceful *peet-sah*; Yellow-bellied offers an even *che-bunk*.

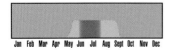

Jan Feb Mar Apr May Jun Jul Aug Sept Oct Nov Dec

Quick ID: sparrow-sized; sexes similar; olive green overall; faint white eye ring; two wing bars; dark bill; yellow wash on belly; dark wings and tail.

Size: 5–6 in.

Eastern Phoebe

Sayornis phoebe

Although many birds pump their tails while they are perched, no bird can match the zest and frequency of the Eastern Phoebe's tail wag. This early spring migrant might lack a distinctive plumage, but its identity is never questioned when the quick and jerky tail rises and falls. Keeping in perfect synchrony with its rhythmic rump, the Eastern Phoebe's voice joins in accompaniment—as its name suggests, this small flycatcher bolts out a cheery *fee-bee* from an exposed spring perch.

The Eastern Phoebe frequently builds its nest on buildings. Phoebes might re-use the same nest site for several years, or they might choose a new site annually. Whatever the case, the Eastern Phoebe's nest is always protected from the rain by a roof—often a bridge, because it likes to nest near streams. If you're lucky, you might even find a phoebe nesting out by your garage or backyard shed!

breeding

Similar Species: Willow Flycatcher (p. 82) and other empidonax flycatchers are smaller and have wing bars. Eastern Wood-Pewee has wing bars and a different voice, and it doesn't wag its tail.

Quick ID: larger than a sparrow; sexes similar; brownish-gray back; no wing bars or eye ring; dark tail, wings and head. *Breeding:* white belly. *Non-breeding:* yellowish belly.
Size: 6¹/₂–7 in.

Jan Feb Mar Apr May Jun Jul Aug Sept Oct Nov Dec

Great Crested Flycatcher

Myiarchus crinitus

The Great Crested Flycatcher is a flycatcher with an attitude. Fitting nicely into the New York scene, this monstrous flycatcher has a loud and assertive whistling call. It can, however, be difficult to observe as it seems habitually to move the instant before binoculars focus upon it.

The Great Crested Flycatcher has an unusual taste in decor for its nest cavity—it occasionally lays a shed snakeskin as a doormat. This uncommon but noteworthy practice can identify the nest of this flycatcher, the only member of its family in New York City to nest in a cavity. The purpose of the snakeskin is not known, but it seems to be important enough that more versatile Great Crested Flycatchers have occasionally substituted plastic wrap or onionskin for reptilian skin.

Similar Species: Eastern Phoebe (p. 83), Eastern Wood-Pewee and other flycatchers are smaller and lack the lemon-yellow belly and the chestnut tail lining.

Jan Feb Mar Apr May Jun Jul Aug Sept Oct Nov Dec

Quick ID: smaller than a robin; sexes similar; yellow belly; gray throat and head; dark back and wings; chestnut tail lining; rufous wing linings; rounded crest.
Size: 7–8 in.

Eastern Kingbird

Tyrannus tyrannus

When one thinks of a tyrant, images of a menacing ruler or a large carnivorous dinosaur are much more likely to come to mind than that of a little bird. Initially, the Eastern Kingbird might not seem as imposing as other known tyrants, but this flycatcher certainly lives up to its scientific name, *Tyrannus tyrannus*. The Eastern Kingbird is pugnacious—it will attack crows, hawks, other large birds and even people that pass through its territory. The intruders are often vigorously pursued, pecked and plucked for some distance until the kingbird is satisfied that there is no further threat.

The courtship flight of the Eastern Kingbird, which can easily be seen in local fields and shrubby areas, is characterized by short, quivering wingbeats. It is a touching display, even for this flattering little tyrant.

Similar Species: Tree Swallow (p. 87) and all other flycatchers lack the white, terminal tail band and are not black and white.

Quick ID: smaller than a robin; sexes similar; black head, back, wings and tail; white underparts; white, terminal tail band; orange-red crown (rarely seen).
Size: 9 in.

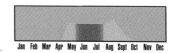

Jan Feb Mar Apr May Jun Jul Aug Sept Oct Nov Dec

Chimney Swift
Chaetura pelagica

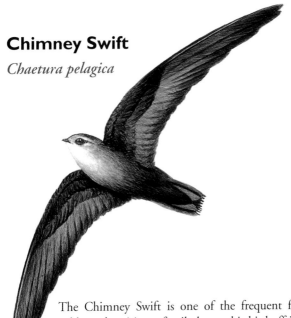

The Chimney Swift is one of the frequent fliers of the bird world—only raising a family keeps this bird off its wings—and it feeds, drinks, bathes and even mates in flight. During its four- to five-year average lifespan, this aeronaut can travel more than one million miles, especially since it winters in South America. Swifts often forage for flying insects at great heights, and during the height of the day they are often visible only as specks in the sky. As the sun sinks to the horizon, however, flocks of Chimney Swifts can be seen spiraling to their evening roosts, casting a distinct boomerang silhouette as they glide.

When they are not in flight, swifts use their small but strong claws to cling precariously to vertical surfaces. Chimney Swifts nest in cavities, and because many old, hollow hardwood trees have been removed over the past few centuries, Chimney Swifts have adopted human structures, such as chimneys, as common nesting sites. Unfortunately, Chimney Swift populations have been declining recently, and it isn't clear whether the problems are on their breeding or wintering grounds.

Similar Species: All swallows have smooth, direct flight and broader wings.

Jan Feb Mar Apr May Jun Jul Aug Sept Oct Nov Dec

Quick ID: smaller than a sparrow; sexes similar; brown overall; slim. *In flight:* rapid wingbeats; erratic flight; boomerang-shaped profile.
Size: 5¹/₂ in.

Tree Swallow

Tachycineta bicolor

Depending on food availability, Tree Swallows might forage for great distances, darting above open fields and wetlands as they catch flying insects in their bills. These bicolored birds occasionally sweep down to the water's surface for a quick mid-flight drink and bath. In bad weather, Tree Swallows might fly up to five miles to distant marshes or lakes to find flying insects in more suitable weather.

The Tree Swallow is among the first migrants to arrive in the New York City area, often beating the onset of warm spring weather. It returns to freshwater marshes by late March to begin its reproductive cycle in early May. It nests in abandoned woodpecker cavities as well as in nest boxes. When the parents leave their eggs for long periods of time, they cover them with feathers to keep them warm. Tree Swallows have such an affinity for feathers when building their nests, that if feathers are tossed into the breeze, the birds will swoop in to catch them.

Similar Species: Chimney Swift (p. 86) has slimmer wings and a darker belly. Bank Swallow has brown upperparts and a brown breast band. Northern Rough-winged Swallow has brown upperparts and a brown wash on the throat.

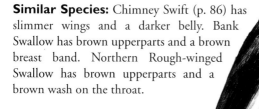

Quick ID: sparrow-sized; sexes similar; white underparts; small bill; small feet. *Adult:* iridescent blue-green upperparts; dark rump. *Immature:* brown upperparts. *In flight:* long, pointed wings; shallowly forked tail.
Size: 5–6 in.

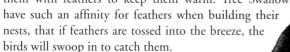

Jan Feb Mar Apr May Jun Jul Aug Sept Oct Nov Dec

Barn Swallow

Hirundo rustica

The Barn Swallow has one of the longest migration routes of any North American land bird—many Barn Swallows winter in Argentina. Despite its long yearly voyage, one cannot imagine a bird better adapted to the challenge. Barn Swallows fly effortlessly, expressing their aerial domination with each stroke of their wings.

The Barn Swallow builds its cup-shaped mud nest in the eaves of barns, picnic shelters or any other structure that provides protection from the rain. It is not uncommon for a nervous parent bird to dive repeatedly at human 'intruders,' encouraging them to retreat, but occasionally a nesting pair of birds can learn to trust their human neighbors, tolerating close, non-threatening visits.

The Barn Swallow is the only swallow in New York City to have a 'swallow tail,' and because it often forages at low altitudes, its deeply forked tail is easily observed.

Similar Species: Purple Martin has a shorter tail and lacks the russet throat and forehead. Cliff Swallow has the same colors overall, but it has a russet rump and a squared-off tail.

Quick ID: large sparrow–sized; sexes similar, but female is a bit duller; deeply forked tail; glossy blue back, wings and tail; buffy underparts; russet throat and forehead.
Size: 6–8 in.

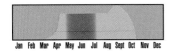

Jan Feb Mar Apr May Jun Jul Aug Sept Oct Nov Dec

Blue Jay

Cyanocitta cristata

The wooded suburbs of New York City and Long Island, with their broken forests and plentiful birdfeeders, must look a lot like Blue Jay heaven. One of our region's most identifiable birds—with its loud *jay-jay-jay* call, its blue, black and white plumage and its large crest—the Blue Jay is familiar to anyone with a generous supply of sunflower seeds, corn or peanuts at their birdfeeder. Blue Jays are intelligent, aggressive and adaptable birds that don't hesitate to drive smaller birds, squirrels or even cats away when they feel threatened.

The Blue Jay represents all the admirable virtues and aggressive qualities of the corvid family, which includes crows and ravens. Beautiful, resourceful and vocally diverse, the Blue Jay can also be one of the most annoying and mischievous birds, and no predator is too formidable for this bird to harass. With their noisy calls, Blue Jays wake up neighborhoods and forests where they are the self-appointed guardians. Fortunately, this colorful bird's extroverted character and boldness outweigh its occasional, briefly annoying behavior.

Similar Species: Eastern Bluebird (p. 100) is smaller, lacks a crest and has a reddish belly.

Quick ID: larger than a robin; sexes similar; blue crest, back, wings and tail; black 'necklace' and lore; white wing bars; light belly.
Size: 11–12 in.

Jan Feb Mar Apr May Jun Jul Aug Sept Oct Nov Dec

American Crow

Corvus brachyrhynchos

It has been suggested that if humans were given feathers and flight, few would be as intelligent as crows. Scientific studies have shown that crows are capable of solving simple problems, which comes as no surprise to anyone who has watched a crow snip open garbage bags with scissors-like precision.

The American Crow calls with the classic, long, descending *caaaw*, either singly or in a series. Throughout the year, this common bird announces the start of the day to New Yorkers. In late summer and fall, when their reproductive duties are completed, crows group together to roost in flocks, known as 'murders.' The crow population seems to have increased in our area, particularly during recent winters, and large flocks can be seen almost anywhere throughout New York City and Long Island.

The New York City area is also home to the virtually identical Fish Crow—a slightly smaller and more coastal-dwelling relative. The Fish Crow is most likely to be seen along the ocean coast scavenging for crustaceans, fish, food waste or the eggs of gulls, terns and herons.

Similar Species: Fish Crow is best distinguished by its more nasal, double-noted *eh-eh* call.

Jan Feb Mar Apr May Jun Jul Aug Sept Oct Nov Dec

Quick ID: small gull–sized; sexes similar; all black; fan-shaped tail.
Size: 18–20 in.

Black-capped Chickadee

Poecile atricapillus

The Black-capped Chickadee is one of the most common and endearing birds of New York City's urban wooded areas. Small, wandering flocks of chickadees seem to go out of their way to greet people strolling through city parks or relaxing in wooded backyards. Brave and adaptable year-round residents, chickadees spend much of the year moving about in loose groups, investigating nooks and crannies for food and uttering their delicate, cheery *chick-a-dee-dee-dee* calls. The chickadees are often joined by other birds, such as nuthatches, kinglets, creepers, Downy Woodpeckers and migrating warblers.

In spring and summer, Black-capped Chickadees seem strangely absent from our city parks and wooded ravines. They tend to remain inconspicuous while they are busily tending to their reproductive duties. Once the first fall chill arrives, however, the woods are once again vibrant with their busy activities and friendly antics.

Similar Species: Tufted Titmouse (p. 92) has a gray crest and lacks the black cap and bib. White-breasted Nuthatch (p. 93) lacks the black chin and has a short tail and a long bill. Blackpoll Warbler (p. 112) is a migrant with orange legs and streaked underparts.

Quick ID: smaller than a sparrow; sexes similar; black cap and bib; white cheeks; grayish back, wings and tail; light underparts.
Size: 5–6 in.

Jan Feb Mar Apr May Jun Jul Aug Sept Oct Nov Dec

Tufted Titmouse

Baeolophus bicolor

On a breaking spring day, an inquisitive Tufted Titmouse whistles *peter peter peter* from its perch, a short flight away from a well-stocked backyard feeder. For much of the year, the Tufted Titmouse is a familiar neighbor in many New York City and Long Island communities—gracing backyards with its trusting inquisitions—although it was rare in our area until the 1950s.

Tufted Titmice can be found nesting in most parks and woodlands. They choose abandoned cavities, previously occupied and excavated by small woodpeckers, in which to build their nests. To make their borrowed homes cozy, titmice line their nests with hair boldly plucked from dogs, wild animals or even humans. If you take the hair accumulated in your hairbrush and set it out in your yard, it might attract a few of these curious birds, who will gladly incorporate a small part of you into the wildness of your neighborhood.

Similar Species: Cedar Waxwing (p. 123) also has a crest, but it is more brown than gray and has a black face mask and a yellow tail tip.

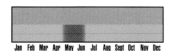

Jan Feb Mar Apr May Jun Jul Aug Sept Oct Nov Dec

Quick ID: sparrow-sized; sexes similar; small crest; dark gray upperparts; light gray underparts; reddish flanks; small black spot on forehead.

Size: 5–6 in.

White-breasted Nuthatch

Sitta carolinensis

Among songbirds, a nuthatch is a bit of an oddball. To the novice birdwatcher, the sight of a White-breasted Nuthatch calling repeatedly while it clings to the underside of a branch might seem out of place. To a nuthatch, however, this gravity-defying act is as natural as flight. These tree-trunk acrobats make their seemingly dangerous headfirst hops look easy and routine. Nuthatches frequently pause in mid-descent, arching their head out at right angles to the trunk and giving their distinctive and often repeated nasal call: *anh-anh-anh-anh.*

White-breasted Nuthatches frequently visit backyard feeders during invasions of Black-capped Chickadees, Tufted Titmice, House Sparrows and Blue Jays. At these busy times, you will notice their brilliant strategy of avoiding conflict: nuthatches rocket in to the feeder, quickly pick out a sunflower seed and then disappear into the surrounding trees. There they scale the bark until they find a crevice in which to store their meal for later consumption. You can also attract nuthatches by hanging a suet feeder from one of your backyard trees during winter.

Similar Species: Black-capped Chickadee (p. 91) has a black bib and a longer tail. Red-breasted Nuthatch has a red breast and a black eye line.

Quick ID: sparrow-sized; white cheek and breast; steel blue back, wings and tail; straight bill; short tail; russet undertail coverts. *Male:* black cap. *Female:* grayish cap.
Size: 6 in.

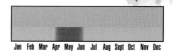

| Jan | Feb | Mar | Apr | May | Jun | Jul | Aug | Sept | Oct | Nov | Dec |

Carolina Wren

Thryothorus ludovicianus

Strong through the southern states, these persistent birds continue to push the limits of their range northward into New York State, blessing New Yorkers with lively singing and chattering. Possibly mating for life, a pair of Carolina Wrens will sing their unique 'duet' year-round as they forage for food and protect their valuable nesting territory.

New York City and Long Island are among the few strongholds of this bird's northern range. In years of mild winter weather, Carolina Wrens become relatively common in New York City. A single cold winter of freezing temperatures and ice-rain can decimate the entire population of Carolina Wrens in New York, forcing them to attempt re-colonization under warmer circumstances. New York City and Long Island residents can help this feathered delight hold its place in our area by maintaining birdfeeders tailored to the tastes of this charming bird—Carolina Wrens are particularly fond of suet and sunflower seeds.

Similar Species: House Wren (p. 95) and Winter Wren lack the prominent white eyebrow. Marsh Wren (p. 96) has a white-streaked, black triangular patch on its back.

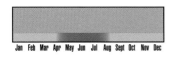

Jan Feb Mar Apr May Jun Jul Aug Sept Oct Nov Dec

Quick ID: sparrow-sized; sexes similar; rusty brown upperparts; deep buff-colored underparts; white throat; long, prominent white eyebrow.
Size: 5 1/2 in.

House Wren

Troglodytes aedon

This common bird of suburbs, city parks and woodlands sings as though its lungs were bottomless. The sweet, warbling song of the House Wren is distinguished by its melodious tone and its uninterrupted endurance. Although the House Wren is far smaller than a sparrow, it offers a seemingly unending song in one breath.

The House Wren is often seen from May to October in woodlands, city parks and backyards, skulking beneath the dense understory. Like all wrens, it frequently carries its short tail cocked straight up. The House Wren treats New York City–area neighborhoods to a few weeks of wonderful warbles in spring before it channels its energy to the task of reproduction. A male House Wren will fill up to a dozen nest boxes or other cavities with twigs for his mate, who will then line one of those nests with grass before laying her eggs.

Similar Species: Carolina Wren (p. 94) is larger and has a white eyebrow. Marsh Wren (p. 96) has white streaking on its back. Winter Wren's tail is shorter than its legs.

Quick ID: small sparrow–sized; sexes similar; brown; tail is often cocked up; slightly down-curved bill; tail is as long as legs.
Size: 5 in.

Jan Feb Mar Apr May Jun Jul Aug Sept Oct Nov Dec

Marsh Wren

Cistothorus palustris

This energetic little bird usually lives in cattail marshes and dense, wet meadows bordered by willows. Although it usually sings from the deep vegetation, its distinctive voice is one of the characteristic sounds of our freshwater wetlands and saltwater marshes. In early spring, Jamaica Bay, Fresh Kills Park and the sheltered marshes protected by Jones Beach ring with the dynamic call of this reclusive bird. Its boisterous song has the repetitive, unnatural quality of an old sewing machine. Once you learn the rhythm, you will hear it whenever you visit many of our local wetlands.

A typical sighting of a Marsh Wren is to spot a brown blur moving noisily about within the shoreline tangles. Although this wren could be less than three yards from the observer, its cryptic habits and appearance are effective camouflage. Patient observers might be rewarded with a brief glimpse of a Marsh Wren perching high atop a cattail reed as it quickly evaluates its territory.

Similar Species: Carolina (p. 94), House (p. 95) and Winter wrens all have unstreaked backs and generally avoid wetlands.

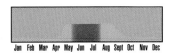

Jan Feb Mar Apr May Jun Jul Aug Sept Oct Nov Dec

Quick ID: smaller than a sparrow; sexes similar; brown overall; white streaking on back; white eye line; light throat and breast; cocked-up tail.
Size: 4–5¹/₂ in.

Golden-crowned Kinglet

Regulus satrapa

The high-pitched, sibilant voice of a Golden-crowned Kinglet is as familiar as the sweet smell of coniferous forests. From October through April, New York City's parks and older, treed communities come alive with the Golden-crowned Kinglet's faint, high-pitched *tsee-tsee-tsee-tsee*.

Although this bird is not immediately obvious to the uninformed passerby, a birdwatcher with a keen ear, patience and the willingness to draw down this smallest of North American songbirds with squeaks and pishes will encounter kinglets on many outdoor trips. As these tiny birds descend in loose flocks around a curious onlooker, their indistinct plumage and voice offer little excitement. When the flock circles nearby, however, flashing their regal crowns as they use the branches as swings and trapezes, the magic of these kinglets will emerge.

Similar Species: Ruby-crowned Kinglet (p. 98) has a reddish crown without a black outline.

Quick ID: smaller than a sparrow; plump; dark olive back; white wing bars; dark tail and wings; white eyebrow. *Male:* fiery orange crown bordered by black. *Female:* lemon yellow crown bordered by black.
Size: 4 in.

Jan Feb Mar Apr May Jun Jul Aug Sept Oct Nov Dec

Ruby-crowned Kinglet

Regulus calendula

Often seen visiting the New York City and Long Island area at the same time as its Golden-crowned relative, the Ruby-crowned Kinglet briefly graces our parks and backyards, especially those with coniferous trees. These birds quickly pass through our area in April, and again from late September to mid-November, always appearing nervous, with their tails and wings flicking continuously as they hop from branch to branch in search of insects.

The Ruby-crowned Kinglet is similar to the Golden-crowned Kinglet in size, habits and coloration, but it has a hidden ruby crown. 'Rubies' are heard more often then they are seen, especially during their spring migration. Their distinctive song starts like a motor chugging to life, and then the kinglets fire off a series of loud, rising *chewy-chewy-chewy-chewy*s. These final phrases are often the only recognizable part of the song.

Similar Species: Golden-crowned Kinglet (p. 97) has a black outline to the crown. Orange-crowned Warbler has no wing bars.

Quick ID: smaller than a sparrow; plump; dark olive; white wing bars; dark tail and wings; incomplete eye ring. *Male:* red crown (infrequently seen). *Female:* no red crown.
Size: 4 in.

Jan Feb Mar Apr May Jun Jul Aug Sept Oct Nov Dec

Blue-gray Gnatcatcher
Polioptila caerulea

♂

breeding

The tails of Blue-gray Gnatcatchers are almost as long as their bodies, and they constantly wave their tails lazily from side to side during their tree-top foraging. Even in soft winds, the Gnatcatcher's tail catches the breeze, and appears to nearly topple the small bird. Gnatcatchers are energetic birds that flit out to catch flying insects, or bounce along branches looking for prey. Although they doubtlessly eat gnats, these insects do not represent a substantial portion of their diet.

Blue-gray Gnatcatchers are noisy nesters, seeming to be totally oblivious of their human neighbors as they constantly issue their familiar *spee* notes. Each pair builds its small nest in a densely foliated deciduous tree, usually close to a source of water. Both sexes help build the structure, cleverly concealing its identity by plastering the outside walls with lichens and spider silk. Although these delightful birds do not seem to be abundant in our area, a larger population is doing well north of the city in Westchester and Orange counties.

Similar Species: Ruby-crowned Kinglet (p. 98) and Golden-crowned Kinglet (p. 97) are olive green overall, with short tails and wing bars. Gray Catbird (p. 120) is much larger and has red undertail coverts.

Quick ID: smaller than a sparrow; long tail; white eye ring; off-white underparts; no wing bars; tail is black above with white outer tail feathers. *Breeding male:* dark blue-gray upperparts; black border to crown. *Female:* light gray upperparts.
Size: 4¹/₂ in.

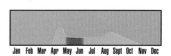

Jan Feb Mar Apr May Jun Jul Aug Sept Oct Nov Dec

Eastern Bluebird

Sialia sialis

Dressed with the colors of the cool sky on his back and the warm setting sun on his breast, the male Eastern Bluebird looks like a piece of pure sky come to life. To fully appreciate this lovely bird, try to spot a male as he sets up his territory on a crisp, early spring morning. Look for our state bird in open country in the more rural setting of Westchester County, north of the city.

The Eastern Bluebird lost many of its natural nesting sites to House Sparrows and European Starlings and to the removal of dead trees throughout New York State. Concerned residents rallied for this bird, however, and they put up thousands of nest boxes to compensate for the losses. The Eastern Bluebird population has slowly increased as a result, and the vigilant residents have been rewarded with the regular sight of this bird's beautiful plumage against the local landscape.

Similar Species: Male Indigo Bunting (p. 142) lacks the red breast and has a conical bill. Blue Jay (p. 89) has a crest and is blue, black and white. Tree Swallow (p. 87), which often nests in bluebird boxes, has an iridescent blue-green back and white underparts.

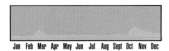

Jan Feb Mar Apr May Jun Jul Aug Sept Oct Nov Dec

Quick ID: smaller than a robin; thin bill; white undertail coverts. *Male:* blue back; red throat and breast. *Female:* less intense colors.
Size: 6–7 in.

Veery

Catharus fuscescens

Like a tumbling waterfall, the Veery's voice descends with a liquid ripple. Like all other thrushes, it is a master of melodies, and it offers its unequaled songs to forests darkening as the sun sets. Listen for its musical treat in Central, Prospect or Van Cortlandt parks during mid-May.

The Veery is perhaps the most terrestrial of New York's thrushes, and it frequently nests on the ground. In characteristic thrush style, it searches for grubs and caterpillars by shuffling through loose leaf litter. When it finds an invertebrate delicacy, the Veery swallows it quickly and, ever-vigilant, cautiously looks about before renewing the hunt.

Similar Species: Wood (p. 102), Hermit and Swainson's thrushes and Ovenbird (p. 115) are more boldly patterned on the breast, each has a characteristic song and none has the uniformly rufous upperparts from the head through the tail.

Quick ID: smaller than a robin; sexes similar; reddish-brown head, back, rump and tail; faint spotting on throat; inconspicuous eye ring.
Size: 7–8 in.

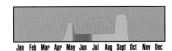

Jan Feb Mar Apr May Jun Jul Aug Sept Oct Nov Dec

Wood Thrush

Hylocichla mustelina

The Wood Thrush was once the voice of Manhattan and Long Island's hardwood forests, embodying the wild spirit of the East, long before the time of traffic jams, concrete jungles and towering skyscrapers. Fortuitously, the Wood Thrush's musical warble—*Will you live with me? Way up high in a tree, I'll come right down and ... seeee!*—is still a common and exhilarating woodland sound throughout much of the rest of New York State. Even in the New York City area, the woods of Staten Island, northern Nassau County and Bronx County still chime with the sweet melodies of this dashing creature.

But life for this bird is no longer as easy as it used to be. Broken, fragmented forests now invite a number of common open-area predators, scavengers and parasites, such as the skunk, fox, crow, jay and cowbird. These animals traditionally had little access to Wood Thrush nests because the nests were insulated deep within the protected confines of vast hardwood forests.

Similar Species: Veery (p. 101) and Swainson's Thrush lack the bold black chest spots and the reddish head. Ovenbird (p. 115) has brown upperparts and a russet crown bordered by black. Hermit Thrush lacks the black spots on the breast and has a reddish rump and tail.

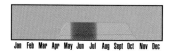

Jan Feb Mar Apr May Jun Jul Aug Sept Oct Nov Dec

Quick ID: smaller than a robin; sexes similar; large black spots on white breast; reddish-brown head, rump and tail; white eye ring; plump.
Size: $7^1/_2$–$8^1/_2$ in.

American Robin

Turdus migratorius

If not for its abundance, the American Robin's voice and plumage would inspire pause and praise from casual onlookers. Acclimatization has dealt the robin an unfair hand, however, and this bird is under-appreciated for the pleasures it offers the eyes and ears of New Yorkers. A robin dashing around a yard in search of worms or ripe berries is as familiar to many people as its three-part *cheerily-cheery up-cheerio* song. Nevertheless, the American Robin's close relationship with urban areas has allowed many residents an insight into a bird's life. Their lively songs, their spotted young and occasionally even their deaths are experiences shared by their human neighbors.

American Robins spend the entire year in the New York City region, but they are sometimes rare from December to late February. Unnoticed by most New Yorkers, the neighborhood robins take seasonal shifts: a few new birds arrive from the north just as most of the summer residents depart for southern climes in fall.

Similar Species: Other thrushes can resemble an immature robin, but robins always have at least a hint of red in the breast.

Quick ID: smaller than a jay; dark head, back and tail; yellow bill; striped throat; white undertail coverts. *Male:* brick red breast; darker hood. *Female:* slightly more orange breast; lighter hood. **Size:** 9–11 in.

Jan Feb Mar Apr May Jun Jul Aug Sept Oct Nov Dec

White-eyed Vireo

Vireo griseus

The bold three- to nine-note song—*quick! pick-up the beer, quick!*—of this uncommon vireo snaps above the vibrant early spring blossoms of the New York City area. Like its vireo kin, the White-eyed Vireo can be a challenge to spot as it dashes and darts through dense brambles and thickets searching for tasty insects or an attractive mate. However, if the bird perches conspicuously, allowing for a brief glance, its glassy white eye will mysteriously draw your attention and confirm the bird's identity.

Even more secretive than the bird itself is the location of its precious nest. Intricately woven out of materials that often include grasses, twigs, bark, lichens, moss, plant down, leaves and the fibrous paper from a wasp nest, the vireo nest is hung between the forking branches of a tree or shrub. Pishing or squeaking observers wandering through Staten Island, Jamaica Bay or southern Westchester County vegetation might receive a brief view and associated scolding from this energetic sprite.

Similar Species: Red-eyed Vireo (p. 105) and Warbling Vireo lack the wing bars and 'spectacles.' Blue-winged Warbler (p. 106), Pine Warbler and Yellow-throated Vireo have yellow throats. Blue-headed Vireo has white 'spectacles,' dark eyes and yellow wing bars.

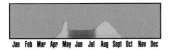

Jan Feb Mar Apr May Jun Jul Aug Sept Oct Nov Dec

Quick ID: small sparrow–sized; sexes similar; yellow 'spectacles'; olive-gray upperparts; white underparts with yellow sides and flanks; whitish wing bars; black pupils in whitish eyes.
Size: 5 in.

Red-eyed Vireo

Vireo olivaceus

The Red-eyed Vireo is the undisputed champion of singing endurance. During the breeding season, males sing from tall deciduous trees throughout the day. While most songbirds stop their courting melodies five or six hours after sunrise, the Red-eyed Vireo seems to gain momentum as the day progresses. One patient ornithologist estimated that the Red-eyed Vireo sings its memorable phrase—*look up, way up, treetop, see me, here-I-am!*—10,000 to 20,000 times a day!

Visual identification of the Red-eyed Vireo is difficult, because its olive-brown color conceals it well among the foliage of deciduous trees. Although this vireo does indeed have red eyes, that feature can only be seen through powerful binoculars in excellent light conditions. Your best clue is to look for the white eyebrow and gray crown separated by a black line.

Similar Species: White-eyed Vireo (p. 104) and Blue-headed Vireo have wing bars and white 'spectacles.' Warbling Vireo lacks the black line and the gray crown above the white eyebrow.

Quick ID: sparrow-sized; sexes similar; gray crown bordered by black; white eyebrow; green back; white underparts; red eyes.
Size: 6 in.

Jan Feb Mar Apr May Jun Jul Aug Sept Oct Nov Dec

Blue-winged Warbler

Vermivora pinus

The blazing yellow Blue-winged Warbler breeds in the New York City area, with breeding pairs regularly reported in the thickets, clearings and woodland edges of southern Westchester and northern Nassau counties. A stroll through Central, Prospect or Van Cortlandt parks during the first two weeks of May should produce an inspirational meeting with these lively, attractive birds moving through in migration.

As recently as the mid-1800s, the Blue-winged Warbler began to move eastward from its mid-western stronghold. The Golden-winged Warbler —a bird with similar habitat requirements and breeding biology— expanded into New York at about the same time, and these two species interbreed in many parts of their range. Just north of New York City, in Orange County, there is a good chance you will see one of the two distinctive, fully fertile hybrids that are occasionally produced.

Similar Species: Yellow Warbler (p. 108) lacks the black mask and the blue-gray wings. Golden-winged Warbler has a dark throat and white underparts. 'Brewster's Warbler' (hybrid) does not have as pure yellow underparts and might have bright yellow wing bars and a gray mantle. 'Lawrence's Warbler' (hybrid) has a black throat, a black mask and yellow underparts.

breeding

Quick ID: smaller than a sparrow; yellow body; black eye line; blue-gray wings and tail; two light wing bars; dark legs. *Male:* brighter yellow on crown. *Female:* yellow-green on head and nape; duller overall.
Size: 4–4³/₄ in.

Jan Feb Mar Apr May Jun Jul Aug Sept Oct Nov Dec

Northern Parula

Parula americana

breeding

♂

♀

This lovely bird is a common spring and fall migrant that can be seen zipping through treetop branches in forested parklands throughout the New York City area. Central, Van Cortlandt and Riverside parks and Jamaica Bay are all excellent places to meet the Northern Parula as it passes through on its way to more northerly nesting grounds in the Adirondack Mountains and beyond.

As warm summer nights slip away to be replaced by cooler fall temperatures, the Northern Parula returns to the warmer climes of Central America. Because it spends most of the year in southern Latin countries, it would most likely sing its cheerful, high, rising song *en Español*, if it could sing with words.

Similar Species: Yellow-rumped Warbler (p. 110) has a yellow crown and rump and a streakier back. White-eyed Vireo (p. 104) has 'spectacles' and lacks the yellow throat. Blue-winged Warbler (p. 106) has yellow undersides. Cerulean Warbler lacks the white eye ring and any yellow color, and has streaking on its breast and sides.

Quick ID: smaller than a sparrow; sexes similar; blue-gray upperparts; white wing bars; broken white eye ring; yellow chin and throat; white belly and flanks; olive patch on back.
Size: 4¹/₂ in.

Jan Feb Mar Apr May Jun Jul Aug Sept Oct Nov Dec

Yellow Warbler

Dendroica petechia

♂

♀

breeding

The Yellow Warbler is common in willow trees, shrublands and brushy areas surrounding wetlands. From late April through to early September, this brilliantly colored warbler is easily found in appropriate habitats throughout our area. As a consequence of its abundance, it is usually the first warbler birdwatchers identify in their lives—and the first they see every spring thereafter.

Yellow Warblers migrate to the tropics for the winter, spending October to April in Central and South America. Following the first warm days of spring, the first Yellow Warblers return to our area, and their distinctive courtship song—*sweet-sweet-sweet I'm so-so sweet!*—is easily recognized despite the birds' seven-month absence. In true warbler fashion, the summertime activities of the Yellow Warbler are energetic and inquisitive: it flits from branch to branch in search of juicy caterpillars, aphids and beetles.

Similar Species: Blue-winged Warbler (p. 106) has a black eye line and a blue-gray tail and wings. Female Common Yellowthroat (p. 116) is not as bright, especially on the face. Wilson's Warbler has a small black cap.

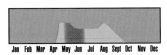

Jan Feb Mar Apr May Jun Jul Aug Sept Oct Nov Dec

Quick ID: smaller than a sparrow; yellow overall; darker back, wings and tail; dark eyes and bill. *Male:* bold red streaking on breast. *Female:* breast is usually unstreaked.
Size: 4–5 in.

Magnolia Warbler

Dendroica magnolia

The Magnolia Warbler is widely regarded as one of the most beautiful wood warblers in North America. Like a customized Cadillac, the Magnolia has all the luxury options: eyebrows, wing bars, a 'necklace,' a yellow rump, throat and belly, tail patches and dark cheeks. As if aware of its stylish beauty, the Magnolia Warbler frequently seems to flaunt its colors to birdwatchers at close range. These beautiful warblers can be seen prancing in the low branches and shrubs during migration as they refuel on newly emerged beetles, flies, wasps and caterpillars.

Birdwatchers have many opportunities to see this glamorous warbler during spring migration at La Tourette, Central, Prospect and Van Cortlandt parks, North Shore Wildlife Sanctuary and Sandy Hook in New Jersey. After a few short weeks in late May, however, all Magnolias will have left our area in favor of cool, northerly spruce and hemlock forests.

Similar Species: Male Yellow-rumped Warbler (p. 110) has a yellow crown and lacks the yellow underparts. Male Cape May Warbler has a rufous cheek. Canada Warbler has solid blue-gray upperparts and yellow 'spectacles' and lacks the yellow rump.

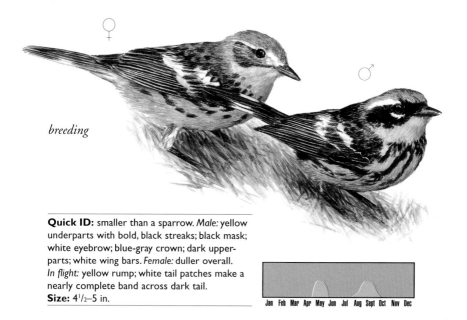

♀

♂

breeding

Quick ID: smaller than a sparrow. *Male:* yellow underparts with bold, black streaks; black mask; white eyebrow; blue-gray crown; dark upperparts; white wing bars. *Female:* duller overall. *In flight:* yellow rump; white tail patches make a nearly complete band across dark tail.
Size: 4¹/₂–5 in.

Jan Feb Mar Apr May Jun Jul Aug Sept Oct Nov Dec

Yellow-rumped Warbler

Dendroica coronata

This spirited songbird is as common as it is delightful. Its contrasting colors, curiosity and tinkling trill are enthusiastically admired by birdwatchers. The Yellow-rumped Warbler is the only warbler in the New York City area that can be found during winter. In fact, it is from late August to mid-May that Yellow-rumps are most noticeable. Insectivorous during the breeding season, these birds survive chilly Long Island winters wherever there is a good crop of bayberries to provide sustenance and insulative red cedar to provide shelter. Spring migrations are especially grand when the trees in local parks and neighborhoods come alive with these colorful, musical birds.

Most experienced birdwatchers call these birds 'Myrtle Warblers,' because they feed on myrtle berries (as well as bayberries) in fall and winter. Until fairly recently, our white-throated form of the Yellow-rumped Warbler was considered a separate species from the western, yellow-throated form (called the 'Audubon's Warbler'). In recognition of the bird's eastern roots and distinct plumage, many birders remain defiant of the name change.

Similar Species: Magnolia Warbler (p. 109) has yellow underparts and white tail patches.

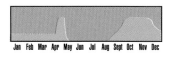

Jan Feb Mar Apr May Jun Jul Aug Sept Oct Nov Dec

Quick ID: sparrow-sized; blue-black back, tail and wings; yellow rump, shoulder patches and crown; white throat; faint white wing bars; dark breast band; white belly; dark cheek. *Male:* bright colors. *Female:* less intense colors.

Size: 5–6 in.

Black-throated Green Warbler

Dendroica virens

breeding

To the sensitive eyes and ears of naturalists, the spring movement of warblers through Central Park is as colorful as Times Square and as melodious as the finest Broadway musical. During May, dozens of species, including the Black-throated Green Warbler, pass through this celebrated urban oasis.

Motivated by the spectacular concentration of songbirds, New Yorkers have long enjoyed birdwatching. Groups such as the New York City Audubon Society have contributed greatly to the development and acceptance of this recreational pursuit. Although New York may not superficially appear a hotbed for naturalists, this community has done much to promote birding activities and make them accessible to a larger audience.

Similar Species: Bay-breasted Warbler has a chestnut throat and lacks the yellow face. Cape May Warbler has a chestnut cheek and yellow and black–streaked underparts.

Quick ID: small sparrow–sized; yellow face; black throat; olive back; dark wings and tail; white wing bars. *Male:* larger black bib.
Size: 5 in.

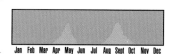

Jan Feb Mar Apr May Jun Jul Aug Sept Oct Nov Dec

Blackpoll Warbler

Dendroica striata

breeding

Blackpolls, which weigh less than a wet tea bag, are champion migrants among warblers. They pass through New York City on their way between South America and their breeding grounds in the Adirondacks and northern Canada. Unlike other warblers, which choose a landlocked migratory passage, Blackpolls shortcut their fall journey by flying south over the Atlantic Ocean, leaving land at Cape Cod and Long Island, and not landing again until they reach the coast of northern Venezuela.

During their spring migration, the bold breeding plumage of Blackpolls allows for easy identification. They pass through our area quite commonly at this time of year, but their activities are infrequently noticed because they generally fly at night and forage among the high treetops. When cold, foggy weather and rains strike New York City in mid- to late May, Blackpoll Warblers are often grounded in Central, Prospect and Van Cortlandt parks, impatiently waiting in the trees for the weather to turn bright.

Similar Species: Black-and-white Warbler (p. 113) has dark legs and a striped, black-and-white crown. Black-capped Chickadee (p. 91) has dark legs and lacks the streaks on its flanks.

Quick ID: sparrow-sized; two white wing bars; orange legs. *Breeding male:* black cap and upperparts; white cheek; black-streaked underparts. *Breeding female:* streaked, greenish upperparts; black-streaked or white underparts; dirty cheek. *Fall adult:* greenish-gray, streaky crown, back and breast.
Size: 5¹/₂ in.

Jan Feb Mar Apr May Jun Jul Aug Sept Oct Nov Dec

Black-and-white Warbler

Mniotilta varia

The foraging behavior of the Black-and-white Warbler lies in sharp contrast to most of its kin. Rather than dancing quickly between twig perches like most warblers, Black-and-white Warblers have a foraging strategy similar to an entirely unrelated group of birds—the nuthatches. As if envious of nuthatches, Black-and-white Warblers hop gingerly up and down tree trunks in search of insect eggs, larval insects, beetles, spiders and other invertebrates.

Black-and-white Warblers occur regularly throughout our area in migration, appearing in wooded backyards and parks. A few birds even remain to breed in surrounding counties, including southern Westchester and northern Nassau. A novice birdwatcher can easily identify this two-toned and oddly behaved warbler. A keen ear also helps: the gentle oscillating song—like a wheel in need of greasing—is easily identified and remembered.

Similar Species: Blackpoll Warbler (p. 112) has orange legs and a solid black cap.

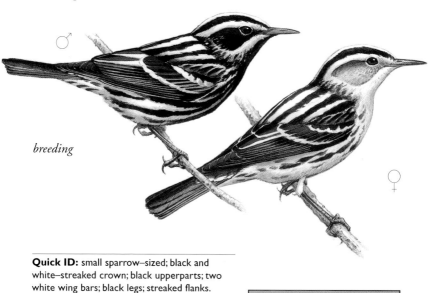

breeding

Quick ID: small sparrow–sized; black and white–streaked crown; black upperparts; two white wing bars; black legs; streaked flanks.
Breeding male: black cheek and throat.
Breeding female: gray cheek; white throat.
Size: 4¹/₂–5¹/₂ in.

Jan Feb Mar Apr May Jun Jul Aug Sept Oct Nov Dec

American Redstart

Setophaga ruticilla

Like an over-energized wind-up toy, the American Redstart flits from branch to branch in a dizzying pursuit of prey. Even while it is perched, its tail gently waves or quickly flicks open and closed, flashing its colorful orange (male) or yellow (female) tail patches. This erratic and amusing behavior is easily observed on this bird's summering ground, as well as in its Central American wintering habitat, where it is affectionately known as *candelita* (little candle). With constantly quivering wings, tail and shoulders, the Redstart's patches provide sparks of life in any dark forest.

Although American Redstarts are one of the most common warblers to pass through the New York City area, their songs are so wonderfully varied that even after a full spring season, their songs can still linger as a confusing mystery. During the first few weeks of May, take a walk through one of our local woodland parks to discover this bird's unique beauty, energy and enthusiasm.

Similar Species: Red-winged Blackbird (p. 133) is much larger, with no red on its chest or tail. Blackburnian Warbler has an orange throat and face and lacks the orange patches in the wings and tail.

Quick ID: small sparrow–sized. *Male:* black overall; fiery orange patches in wings, tail and side of breast; white belly. *Female:* olive-gray back; light underparts; peach yellow patches in wings, tail and shoulders.
Size: 5 in.

Jan Feb Mar Apr May Jun Jul Aug Sept Oct Nov Dec

Ovenbird

Seiurus aurocapillus

The sharp, loud call of the Ovenbird rises forcefully each spring from the dense shrubs and plants in Central, Bronx and Forest parks. The Ovenbird—or at least its song, *teacher teacher Teacher TEACHER*—is encountered frequently during New York City's refreshing spring mornings. This distinctive, familiar song announces the Ovenbird's presence on its breeding grounds, but not necessarily during migration. Its noisy habit of walking through the dense undergrowth nearly reveals its precise location, but this songbird's cryptic plumage and refusal to become airborne frustrate many birders intent on a quick peek. Ovenbirds rarely expose themselves to the open forest; they seem most comfortable in the tangles of shrubs, stumps and dead leaves.

Efforts to protect and restore the integrity of our last remaining mature deciduous forests will ensure the continued presence of the Ovenbird on Long Island. With the assistance of visionaries, the woodlands will continue to sing each May, just as they have for many millennia.

Similar Species: Wood Thrush (p. 102) and Hermit Thrush are much larger, and they lack the russet crown streak. Veery (p. 101) lacks the large black breast spots and the black border of the crown. Northern Waterthrush lacks the russet crown and has a white eyebrow.

Quick ID: sparrow-sized; sexes similar; heavily streaked breast; bold eye ring; olive-brown back; russet crown bordered by black; orange legs.
Size: 6 in.

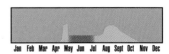

Common Yellowthroat

Geothlypis trichas

With so much diversity within North America's wood warbler family, it is no surprise that one species has forsaken forests in favor of cattail marshes. In our area, this energetic warbler reaches its highest abundance along freshwater wetland brambles and cattails, but it can also be seen and heard even in drier fields and second-growth thickets some distance from water. If you are keen on meeting a colorful, spirited yellowthroat, you should visit the edges of any marshy habitat in the New York City area.

The male Common Yellowthroat is easily identified by his black mask or by his oscillating *witchety-witchety-witchety* song. Female yellowthroats are rarely seen. They quietly keep to their nests deep within the thick, low-growing vegetation. Yellowthroat chicks develop rapidly and soon leave the nest, allowing the parents to raise a second brood. Common Yellowthroat nests are often parasitized by Brown-headed Cowbirds.

Similar Species: Male is distinctive. Female Yellow Warbler (p. 108) has a much brighter body and face. Nashville Warbler has dark brown legs and an eye ring. Female Wilson's Warbler has a yellow eyebrow and the hint of a dark cap.

Quick ID: smaller than a sparrow; orange legs; yellow throat and underparts; olive upperparts. *Male:* black mask with white border on forehead. *Female:* plain face (no mask).
Size: 4¹/₂–5¹/₂ in.

Jan Feb Mar Apr May Jun Jul Aug Sept Oct Nov Dec

Scarlet Tanager

Piranga olivacea

breeding

The tropical appearance of the male Scarlet Tanager's plumage reinforces the link between the forests of South America and those of eastern North America. A winter resident of the tropics and a breeder in New York City's mature deciduous woods, this tanager is vulnerable to deforestation at both extremes of its range.

Despite their blazing red plumage, Scarlet Tanagers can be difficult to see, mainly because they tend to stay high up in forest canopies. They sing a robin-like warble—*hurry-worry-lurry-scurry!*—that is all too frequently disregarded as coming from that more familiar woodland voice. Careful listeners will note that the song is shorter and burrier than a robin's, and even novice birdwatchers can listen for the tanager's unique hiccup-like *chick-burr* call. If you are lucky, you might happen upon a tanager foraging close to the ground during rainy or foggy weather, particularly among the low foliage of Central, Forest or Van Cortlandt parks during May or late September migration.

Similar Species: Northern Cardinal (p. 140) has a crest, a heavy bill and red wings. Male Baltimore Oriole (p. 137) is black and orange. Male Orchard Oriole is black and chestnut. Both male orioles have black heads. Female orioles have thinner bills and wing bars.

Quick ID: larger than a sparrow. *Breeding male:* unmistakable, magnificent scarlet body; black wings and tail. *Non-breeding male:* yellow-green body; black wings and tail. *Female:* olive-yellow overall; no wing bars.
Size: 6¹/₂–7¹/₂ in.

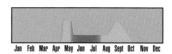

Jan Feb Mar Apr May Jun Jul Aug Sept Oct Nov Dec

Horned Lark

Eremophila alpestris

Horned Larks are probably most frequently encountered rising up in front of vehicles speeding along country roads. They cut off to the side of cars the instant before a fatal collision occurs, briefly showing off their distinct, white outer feathers on a black tail. Horned Larks resort to these near-misses because their first instinct when threatened is to outrun their pursuer. Because cars can easily overtake these swift runners, they take to the air when their first attempt to flee fails.

Winter is a good time to see large flocks of larks feeding on seeds and waste grain in country fields. Most of the larks wintering in New York are destined to migrate north when the first hints of warmth loosen winter's chilly grip. This does not mean, however, that our area is free of these birds through summer, because many larks nest in our open fields and pastures. They are among the earliest of our courting birds, singing their songs and diving dare-devilishly to the ground during February and March.

Similar Species: Sparrows lack the black facial and throat markings.

♂

Jan Feb Mar Apr May Jun Jul Aug Sept Oct Nov Dec

Quick ID: larger than most sparrows; sexes similar (female slightly lighter-colored); brown plumage; black bib, mask and 'tiara'; light underparts; black tail with white outer tail feathers; faint yellow throat.
Size: 7–8 in.

European Starling

Sturnus vulgaris

breeding

In April 1890, after several attempts to introduce European Starlings to New York City, 60 of these birds were released in Central Park. These birds quickly established themselves in the New York City landscape, and North America has never been the same since. Within a century, this European bird has spread across most of the continent, often producing massive wintering flocks that can exceed one million birds.

Unfortunately, the expansion of starlings has come at the expense of many of our native birds, including the Purple Martin and the Eastern Bluebird, which are unable to defend their nest cavities against the aggressive starlings. Few birdwatchers are pleased with the presence of this foreigner to our area, but starlings have become a permanent fixture in the bird community. If residents are unable to find joy in this bird's remarkable mimicry and astounding flocking behavior, they can take some comfort knowing that starlings now provide a reliable and stable food source for a variety of woodland hawks, Merlins and New York City's own Peregrine Falcons.

Similar Species: All blackbirds have longer tails and black bills. Purple Martin has a short bill.

Quick ID: smaller than a robin; sexes similar; short tail. *Breeding:* dark, glossy plumage; long, yellow bill. *Non-breeding:* dull bill; spotty plumage. *Juvenile:* dull gray-brown overall; brown bill.
Size: 8–9 in.

Jan Feb Mar Apr May Jun Jul Aug Sept Oct Nov Dec

Gray Catbird

Dumetella carolinensis

The Gray Catbird is a sleek bird that commonly displays an unusual 'mooning' behavior—it raises its long, slender tail to show its chestnut undertail coverts. This behavior is one of the elements of courtship, and the coverts might help female catbirds choose the best mates.

The Gray Catbird is a bird of dense shrubs and thickets, and although it's relatively common in appropriate habitats, its distinctive call, rather than the bird itself, is what most people commonly encounter. The Gray Catbird's unmistakable, cat-like 'meowing,' for which it is named, can be heard rising from shrubs and thickets throughout the city, especially from early May through to September.

Similar Species: Female Brown-headed Cowbird (p. 136) has lightly streaked underparts and lacks the black cap and chestnut undertail coverts, and its bill is thicker at the base.

Jan Feb Mar Apr May Jun Jul Aug Sept Oct Nov Dec

Quick ID: smaller than a robin; sexes similar; slate gray body; black cap; chestnut undertail coverts; long, dark tail.
Size: 9 in.

Northern Mockingbird

Mimus polyglottos

Considered a rare and erratic summer resident throughout the New York City area until the 1950s, the Northern Mockingbird is now a common year-round resident throughout much of southeastern New York State. As human development blossomed along the Eastern Seaboard, mockingbirds began to push northward into the New York City area. Over time, with the help of consistently mild winter weather in our region since 1955, the creation of broken forest habitats and the planting of urban fruit-bearing trees and shrubs, these fascinating birds have established themselves as a permanent fixture in our urban and rural communities.

The Northern Mockingbird is perhaps best known for its ability to mimic sounds. It will expertly imitate other birds, barking dogs and even musical instruments in its seeming quest to expand the size and diversity of its vocal repertoire. Scientific evidence suggests that mockingbirds with larger, more complex repertoires are better at attracting mates and intimidating nearby competitors.

Similar Species: Loggerhead Shrike has a black mask and a stout, hooked bill.

Quick ID: robin-sized; sexes similar; white patches in dark wings; dark tail with white outer tail feathers; gray head and back; light underparts; long tail; thin bill.
Size: 10 in.

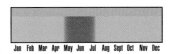

Jan Feb Mar Apr May Jun Jul Aug Sept Oct Nov Dec

Brown Thrasher

Toxostoma rufum

Male Brown Thrashers have the largest vocal repertoire of any New York City–area bird—more than 3000 song types. Although thrashers don't possess the sweetest voices in New York City, their loud, continually varying songs are definitely worth a listen. Thrashers will repeat phrases twice, often combining them into complex choruses, such as *dig-it dig-it, hoe-it hoe-it, pull-it-up pull-it-up.*

Brown Thrashers are generally easy to identify among the other birds found in New York City–area communities. Look for the unmistakable combination of a long, downcurved bill, reddish-brown back, long reddish-brown tail and heavily streaked breast. They're found in the sparse patches of thickets and shrubs, often in fairly close proximity to humans. They're shy birds, however, and they need a lot of coaxing with squeaks and pishes before they pop out into the open. In spring and summer, Jamaica Bay and Fresh Kills Park offer good opportunities to meet this dynamic songster.

Similar Species: Wood Thrush (p. 102) and Veery (p. 101) both have shorter tails and straight bills.

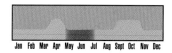

Jan Feb Mar Apr May Jun Jul Aug Sept Oct Nov Dec

Quick ID: jay-sized; sexes similar; reddish-brown head, back and long tail; heavy chest streaking; long, downcurved bill; white wing bars; no eye ring.
Size: 11–12 in.

Cedar Waxwing

Bombycilla cedrorum

A faint, high-pitched, buzzy trill is often your first clue that waxwings are around. If you hear this sound, quickly scan the skies or neighborhood treetops to see these cinnamon-crested birds plying the skies in large flocks or darting out from tree limbs to snack on flying insects.

Cedar Waxwings are found in many habitats throughout New York City—wherever ripe berries provide abundant food supplies. They are most often seen in large flocks in late spring and early fall, when they can quickly eat all the berries on fruit trees. Some people remember these visits not only for the birds' beauty, but because fermentation of the fruit occasionally renders the flock flightless from intoxication.

Similar Species: Tufted Titmouse (p. 92) lacks the black face mask and the yellow in its belly.

Quick ID: smaller than a robin; sexes similar; fine, pale, silky-brown plumage; small crest; black mask; yellow belly wash; yellow-tipped tail; light undertail coverts; shiny red (waxy-looking) droplets on wing tips.
Size: 7–8 in.

Jan Feb Mar Apr May Jun Jul Aug Sept Oct Nov Dec

Eastern Towhee

Pipilo erythrophthalmus

This large, cocky sparrow is most often heard scratching away leaves and debris under dense shrubs and bushes long before it is seen. Among the deep shadows of shrubs, the Eastern Towhee's sharp *Drink your Teeea* positively identifies this secretive sparrow. To observe this bird, it is best to learn a few birding tricks—squeaking and pishing are irresistible sounds for towhees. Towhees will soon pop out from cover to investigate the noise, revealing their surprising combination of colors.

The Eastern Towhee is a summer resident of pine barrens, brambles and forest openings like those found in Jamaica Bay, Jones Beach and La Tourette Park. It was formerly grouped together with the western Spotted Towhee as a single species: the Rufous-sided Towhee.

Similar Species: American Robin (p. 103) is larger and has no white on its chest. Dark-eyed Junco (p. 131) is smaller and has completely white outer tail feathers, rather than just white tail corners.

Quick ID: smaller than a robin; black head and back; rufous-colored flanks; white outer tail corners; white underparts; red eyes. *Male:* black head, breast and upperparts. *Female:* brown head, breast and upperparts.
Size: 8–9 in.

Jan Feb Mar Apr May Jun Jul Aug Sept Oct Nov Dec

Chipping Sparrow

Spizella passerina

Hopping around freshly mowed lawns, the cheery Chipping Sparrow goes about its business unconcerned by the busy world of suburban New York City and Long Island. One of New York's most widespread species, the Chipping Sparrow brings birdwatching to those who rarely venture from their homes. They demand nothing more than a little privacy around an ornamental conifer where they have chosen to nest.

Chipping Sparrows frequently nest in our backyards, but not in the heart of the city—they need at least a lawn and a few ornamental trees. They build their small nest cups with dried vegetation and line them with animal hair. Chipping Sparrows usually attempt to bring up two broods every year—they lay three or four small, greenish-blue eggs in mid-May and later near the beginning of July, should conditions prove favorable.

Similar Species: Field Sparrow (p. 124) has a pink bill and a gray eyebrow. American Tree Sparrow is only a winter resident and has a black central chest spot.

breeding

Quick ID: small sparrow; sexes similar; red crown; white eyebrow; black eye line; clear, whitish-gray breast; streaked back.
Size: 5¹/₂ in.

Jan Feb Mar Apr May Jun Jul Aug Sept Oct Nov Dec

Field Sparrow

Spizella pusilla

The innocent, unmarked face of the Field Sparrow gives this common bird a perpetual look of adolescence. Like a teenage boy prior to his first shave, the Field Sparrow has a soft, wholesome look, highlighted by its pink bill and untainted eyes.

Many sparrows have very descriptive and accurate names, but the Field Sparrow's name is somewhat misleading. An inhabitant of overgrown meadows and bushy areas—which seem to be decreasing in our area—the Field Sparrow tends to avoid open, expansive, grassy fields. These birds have adapted well to the shrubby growth in clearings below power lines.

Field Sparrows often nest far away from human developments, but not far enough from Brown-headed Cowbirds, which can parasitize more than one-quarter of the nests in our area, affecting this sparrow's reproductive success. Field Sparrow populations have declined in the New York City area—habitat loss is probably the primary cause, with cowbird parasitism as a secondary factor.

Similar Species: Chipping Sparrow (p. 125) has a white eyebrow and a black eye line. American Tree Sparrow has a dark chest spot and a dark bill.

Jan Feb Mar Apr May Jun Jul Aug Sept Oct Nov Dec

Quick ID: mid-sized sparrow; sexes similar; reddish crown; plain gray underparts; pink bill; light gray eyebrow; rusty brown back.
Size: 5–6 in.

Saltmarsh Sharp-tailed Sparrow

Ammodramus caudacutus

Differentiating between all those little brown birds known as sparrows can seem like a nightmarish challenge. With the Saltmarsh Sharp-tailed Sparrow, however, all you have to do is look it in the eye to see the unique orange facial triangle. Its streaky, buff-colored breast and sides and its gray ear patch also separate it from many other sparrows. A third clue to this sparrow's identity is its choice of habitat: the tidal saltmarshes of the Long Island coast.

Unlike other sparrow species, breeding Saltmarsh Sharp-tails do not form pair bonds. Males do not defend a breeding territory or help the females raise the young. Instead, a male flies through the marsh, occasionally stopping to attract a mate through song. After mating, the male moves on to search for other potential mates, while the female begins the business of raising the young (or looks for another mate herself).

Similar Species: Field (p. 126), Seaside (p. 128) and Swamp sparrows all lack the orange facial triangle. Nelson's Sharp-tailed Sparrow has much lighter streaking on its breast, flanks and back, and it is only in the New York City area briefly during migration.

Quick ID: small sparrow; sexes similar; buffy breast and flanks streaked with brown; gray ear patch surrounded by orange triangle; gray central crown stripe; unstreaked gray nape.
Size: 5¹/₄ in.

Jan Feb Mar Apr May Jun Jul Aug Sept Oct Nov Dec

Seaside Sparrow

Ammodramus maritimus

In the New York City area, you will only find this sparrow among the tidal saltmarshes of the Long Island coast, primarily along its southern shores from Jamaica Bay to Jones Beach. It is here among the tall stands of cordgrass, blackfoot rush, salt-meadow grass and saltmarsh-elders that the Seaside Sparrow finds everything it needs to survive and breed.

Foraging primarily on the ground, it enjoys a diverse diet of insects, spiders, small aquatic invertebrates and seeds. Meetings with this bird can be brief and seemingly unrewarding, because most flushed birds flutter only a short distance before disappearing into thick vegetation. Fortunate observers might delight in the view of a courting male projecting his cheery song from near the top of the cordgrass or during a courtship flight.

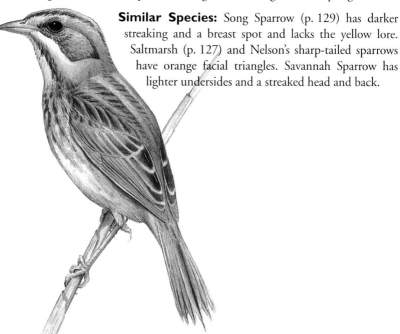

Similar Species: Song Sparrow (p. 129) has darker streaking and a breast spot and lacks the yellow lore. Saltmarsh (p. 127) and Nelson's sharp-tailed sparrows have orange facial triangles. Savannah Sparrow has lighter undersides and a streaked head and back.

Jan Feb Mar Apr May Jun Jul Aug Sept Oct Nov Dec

Quick ID: mid-sized sparrow; sexes similar; flattened forehead blends into thickened bill; yellow lore; gray whisker stripe; olive-gray upperparts; pale gray, lightly streaked underparts.
Size: 6 in.

Song Sparrow
Melospiza melodia

The Song Sparrow's drab, heavily streaked plumage doesn't prepare you for its symphonic song, which stands among the best in the New York City area for complexity and rhythm. This commonly heard bird is one of the first in song during spring, and it seems to bear good news by singing *hip-hip-hip hooray boys, the spring is here again.*

This year-round resident is easily found in a wide variety of habitats: marshes, thickets, brambles, weedy fields and woodland edges. Some birds withdraw during winter, but many continue to be encountered at backyard feeders and parks around the city.

Song Sparrows are most easily identified by their grayish facial streaks while they are perched. Flying birds often characteristically pump their tails, making them look like a comma in flight.

Similar Species: Fox Sparrow is very heavily streaked and has a different song. Savannah Sparrow has a yellow lore. Lincoln's Sparrow has a buffy wash across the breast.

Quick ID: large sparrow; sexes similar; heavy breast streaks form central spot; brown plumage; striped head.
Size: 6–7 in.

Jan Feb Mar Apr May Jun Jul Aug Sept Oct Nov Dec

White-throated Sparrow
Zonotrichia albicollis

The catchy song of the White-throated Sparrow is often on the lips of weekend cottagers returning from the Adirondack wilds. By whistling the distinctive *Old Sam Peabody Peabody Peabody* to themselves, people bring some of the atmosphere of the woods home to the city. This voice of conifer forests is as sure a sign of spring in cottage country as the melting snow and returning cottagers. The White-throat's striped head and white throat allow it to stand out from House Finches and bland sparrow relatives.

In late April, early May and October, thousands of White-throated Sparrows pass through New York City. Many of them stop in Central Park, in Prospect Park and even at backyard feeders to take a breather and catch a quick meal. During winter, too, many of these birds remain to forage for plant seeds or munch on birdfeeder offerings in our parks and backyards.

Similar Species: White-crowned Sparrow has a less conspicuous whitish throat and a pink bill.

Jan Feb Mar Apr May Jun Jul Aug Sept Oct Nov Dec

Quick ID: large sparrow; sexes similar; black-and-white or black-and-tan stripes on head; white throat; unstreaked, light gray breast; yellow lore; rusty brown upperparts.
Size: 6¹/₂–7 in.

Dark-eyed Junco

Junco hyemalis

Dark-eyed Juncos are abundant winter visitors throughout the New York City area. They are ground dwellers, and they are frequently seen flushing from the undergrowth along wooded park trails. Their distinctive, white outer tail feathers flash in alarm as they fly down a narrow, open path before disappearing into a concealing thicket.

Just before departing for their northern breeding grounds in April, Dark-eyed Juncos sing their musical trills, which are easily mistaken with those of the Chipping Sparrow. The junco's distinctive smacking call and its habit of double-scratching at forest litter also help identify it. Juncos are frequent guests at birdfeeders throughout New York City and Long Island, usually preferring to clean up the scraps that have fallen to the ground.

Similar Species: Eastern Towhee (p. 124) is larger and has conspicuous rufous sides. Male Brown-headed Cowbird (p. 136) lacks the white outer tail feathers and the white belly.

Quick ID: mid-sized sparrow; sexes similar (female is somewhat duller); slate gray head and upperparts; white belly; light-colored bill; white outer tail feathers.
Size: 5–6 ¹/₂ in.

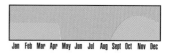

Jan Feb Mar Apr May Jun Jul Aug Sept Oct Nov Dec

Bobolink

Dolichonyx oryzivorus

breeding

In spring, small flocks of Bobolinks pass through New York City on their way to breed in weedy fields north of the city. The males, which look as though they're wearing tuxedos backwards, arrive a few days before the females and perform their bubbly, tinkly song—*bob-o-link bob-o-link, spink, spank, spink*—assuring farmers and naturalists that spring is here to stay.

At first glimpse, Bobolinks look every bit a sparrow, especially the drab females, which lack the males' style. These birds are not sparrows, however, but blackbirds. This kinship is evident in their polygynous breeding strategy, and males that acquire prime hayfields can mate and defend several nesting females.

The fall migration of Bobolinks is a spectacular sight. Flocks leaving the northern coast congregate with others from the west and soon number in the thousands of birds. These flocks historically descended on rice crops in the southeast states to feed, and they were given the name 'rice birds' for their costly appetites. Bobolinks continue south during fall to winter in rice fields in South America.

Similar Species: Brown-headed Cowbird (p. 136) has a black back. Sparrows tend to lack the pointy tail feathers.

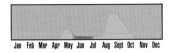

Jan Feb Mar Apr May Jun Jul Aug Sept Oct Nov Dec

Quick ID: large sparrow–sized; pointed tail feathers. *Breeding male:* black head and body; buffy nape; white rump and shoulders. *Female* and *Non-breeding male:* buffy brown body; dark crown streaks; dark eye line.
Size: 6–8 in.

Red-winged Blackbird

Agelaius phoeniceus

From March through July, no marsh is free from the loud calls and bossy, aggressive nature of the Red-winged Blackbird. A springtime walk around Jamaica Bay Wildlife Refuge or through the brush at any wetland or field will be accompanied by this bird's loud, raspy and persistent *konk-a-reee* or *eat my CHEEEzies* song.

The male's bright red shoulders (called 'epaulettes') are his most important tool in the strategic and intricate displays he uses to defend his territory from rivals and to attract a mate. In experiments, males whose red shoulders were painted black soon lost their territories to rivals they had previously defeated. The female's interest lies not in the individual combatants, however, but in the nesting habitat, and a male who can successfully defend a large area of dense cattails will breed with many females. After the females have built their concealed nests and laid their eggs, the male continues his persistent vigil.

Similar Species: Common Grackle (p.135) and Brown-headed Cowbird (p. 136) both lack the red shoulder patches.

Quick ID: smaller than a robin. *Male:* all-black plumage; large red patch bordered by creamy yellow on each shoulder. *Female:* brown overall; heavily streaked; hint of red on shoulder.
Size: 7¹/₂–9¹/₂ in.

Jan Feb Mar Apr May Jun Jul Aug Sept Oct Nov Dec

Eastern Meadowlark

Sturnella magna

The Eastern Meadowlark is well adapted to the landscape of fields and pastures where it spends its summers. Its melodic, flute-like song—*This is the Year*—is a signature of open country. As undisturbed open fields decrease in the New York City area, so too do populations of the Eastern Meadowlark, but it can still be found at Floyd Bennett Field and John F. Kennedy International Airport.

Eastern Meadowlarks are both showy and perfectly camouflaged. Their yellow sweater with the black V-neck and their white outer tail feathers serve to attract mates. Courting meadowlarks face one another, raise their bills high and perform a grassy field ballet. Oddly, the colorful breast and white tail feathers are also used to attract the attention of potential predators. Foxes, hawks or falcons focus on these bold features in pursuit, but then their prey mysteriously disappears into the grass whenever the meadowlark chooses to turn its back or fold away its white tail flags.

Similar Species: None.

breeding

Jan Feb Mar Apr May Jun Jul Aug Sept Oct Nov Dec

Quick ID: robin-sized; sexes similar; mottled brown upperparts; black 'V' on chest; yellow throat and belly; white outer tail feathers; striped head.
Size: 8–10 in.

Common Grackle

Quiscalus quiscula

The Common Grackle is a noisy bird that prefers to feed on the ground in open areas. Birdfeeders in rural areas can attract large numbers of these long-tailed blackish birds, whose cranky and aggressive disposition drives away most other birds. The Common Grackle is easily identified by its long tail, large bill and dark plumage, which can shine with hues of green, purple and blue in bright light.

The Common Grackle is a poor but spirited singer. Usually while perched in a shrub, a male grackle will slowly take a deep breath that inflates his chest and causes his feathers to rise; then he closes his eyes and gives out a loud, surprising *swaaaack*, not unlike a rusty gate. Despite our perception of the Common Grackle's musical weakness, following his 'song,' the male smugly and proudly poses with his bill held high.

Similar Species: Red-winged Blackbird (p. 132) and Brown-headed Cowbird (p. 136) have relatively shorter bills and tails and have dark eyes. American Crow (p. 90) is much larger and bulkier. Rusty Blackbird in fall plumage has a rusty tinge on its head, back and wings, and spring and summer birds are all black and generally lack the multicolored iridescence.

Quick ID: jay-sized; sexes similar; glossy black plumage with purple and bronze iridescence; long tail; yellow eyes; large bill.
Size: 11–13 in.

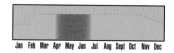

Jan Feb Mar Apr May Jun Jul Aug Sept Oct Nov Dec

Brown-headed Cowbird

Molothrus ater

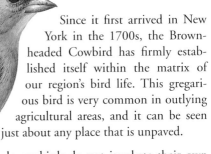

Since it first arrived in New York in the 1700s, the Brown-headed Cowbird has firmly established itself within the matrix of our region's bird life. This gregarious bird is very common in outlying agricultural areas, and it can be seen just about any place that is unpaved.

Female cowbirds do not incubate their own eggs; instead they lay them in the nests of many songbirds. Cowbird eggs have a short incubation period, and the cowbird chicks often hatch before the host songbird's own chicks. Many songbirds will continue to feed the fast-growing cowbird chick even after it has outgrown its surrogate parent. In its efforts to get as much food as possible, a cowbird chick might squeeze the host's own young out of the nest. The populations of some songbirds have been reduced in part by the activities of the Brown-headed Cowbird, but other songbird species recognize the foreign egg, and they either eject it from their nest or they build a new nest.

Similar Species: Common Grackle (p. 135) and Rusty Blackbird have yellow eyes. Female Red-winged Blackbird (p. 133) has much more streaking on its underparts.

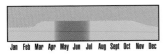

Jan Feb Mar Apr May Jun Jul Aug Sept Oct Nov Dec

Quick ID: smaller than a robin; dark eyes. *Male:* metallic-looking, glossy black plumage; soft brown head. *Female:* brownish gray overall; slight breast streaks.
Size: 6–8 in.

Baltimore Oriole

Icterus galbula

Although it is a common summer resident of city parks and woodlands, the Baltimore Oriole is seldom seen. Unlike the American Robin, which inhabits the human domain of shrubs and lawns, the Baltimore Oriole nests and feeds in the tallest deciduous trees available. This bird's hanging, six-inch-deep, pouch-like nest is deceptively strong, and a vacant nest, which is easily seen on bare trees in fall, is often the only indication that a pair of orioles summered in an area.

From early May to mid-June, the open parklands of Central, Bronx, La Tourette and Brookville parks are among the most productive destinations for oriole-starved New York City birdwatchers. The male Baltimore Oriole's striking, Halloween-like, black-and-orange plumage flashes like embers amidst the dense foliage of the treetops, while his slow, purposeful *Peter Peter here here Peter Peter* song drips down to eager listeners along the forest floor.

Similar Species: Orchard Oriole is smaller and has chestnut, rather than orange, plumage.

Quick ID: smaller than a robin. *Male:* brilliant orange belly, flanks, outer tail feathers and rump; black hood, wings and tail. *Female:* gray-green upperparts; orangish underparts; some have a faint hood.
Size: 7–8 in.

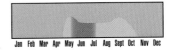

Jan Feb Mar Apr May Jun Jul Aug Sept Oct Nov Dec

House Finch

Carpodacus mexicanus

The House Finch is one of the earliest voices to announce the coming of spring. These common city and country birds sing their melodies from backyards, parks, ivy vines and telephone lines.

During the 1920s and 1930s, this bird, which is native to the American Southwest, was a popular cage bird, and it was sold across the continent as the 'Hollywood Finch.' Illegal releases of the cage birds on Long Island in the 1940s resulted in a wild population, which quickly spread throughout the New York City region and all the way to the Rocky Mountains. The increase of House Finches has recently been reversed, however, because they have become vulnerable to disease. Birds with bald patches or crusty eyes, seen at backyard feeders, often indicate the presence of this disease.

Similar Species: Male Purple Finch is raspberry-colored and has unstreaked undertail coverts, and the female has a brown cheek contrasting with a white eyebrow and a mustache stripe.

Jan Feb Mar Apr May Jun Jul Aug Sept Oct Nov Dec

Quick ID: sparrow-sized. *Male:* deep red forehead, eyebrow and throat; buffy gray belly; brown cheek; streaked sides and undertail coverts. *Female:* brown overall; streaked underparts; lacks prominent eyebrow.
Size: 5–6 in.

American Goldfinch

Carduelis tristis

In spring, the American Goldfinch swings over fields in its distinctive, undulating flight, and it fills the air with its jubilant *po-ta-to chip* call. This bright, cheery songbird is commonly seen during summer in weedy fields, roadsides and backyards, where it often feeds on thistle seeds. The American Goldfinch delays nesting until July, August and even September to ensure a dependable source of insects, thistles and dandelion seeds to feed its young.

The American Goldfinch is a common backyard bird, particularly in Richmond, Westchester and northern Nassau counties, where it is attracted to feeding stations that offer a supply of niger (or 'thistle') seed. Unfortunately, goldfinches are easily bullied at feeders by larger sparrows and finches. Only goldfinches and Pine Siskins invert for food, however, so a special finch feeder with openings below the perches is ideal for ensuring a steady stream of what some people mistakenly call 'wild canaries.'

Similar Species: Yellow Warbler (p. 108) does not have black on its forehead or wings. Evening Grosbeak is much larger and has broad white wing patches.

Quick ID: smaller than a sparrow. *Breeding male:* black forehead, wings and tail; canary yellow body; wings show white in flight. *Female* and *Non-breeding male:* no black on forehead; yellow-green overall; black wings and tail.
Size: 4¹/₂–5¹/₂ in.

Jan Feb Mar Apr May Jun Jul Aug Sept Oct Nov Dec

Northern Cardinal
Cardinalis cardinalis

Never far apart, male and female cardinals softly vocalize to one another year-round, not just through the breeding season. Their ritualized, beak-to-beak feeding reinforces the romantic appeal and bond of these easily identified birds. Although the regal male does little more than warble to the female while she constructs the nest, his parental duties will soon keep him busy. After the eggs have hatched, the nestlings and the brooding female will remain in the nest while the male provides much of the food for the entire family.

People who enjoy feeding birds in the New York City area should not be complacent about their cardinals—this bird disappeared from our area in the early part of the 20th century and did not return until the 1940s. As if grateful to residents with feeders, Northern Cardinals offer up their bubbly *What cheer! What cheer! Birdie-birdie-birdie What cheer!* to awaken New York City neighborhoods.

Similar Species: Male Scarlet Tanager (p. 117) has a black tail and wings and no crest.

Quick ID: smaller than a robin. *Male:* unmistakable; red overall; black mask and throat; pointed crest; red, conical bill. *Female:* considerably duller and browner plumage. *Immature:* like a female, but with a dark bill.
Size: 8–9 in.

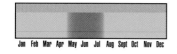

Jan Feb Mar Apr May Jun Jul Aug Sept Oct Nov Dec

Rose-breasted Grosbeak

Pheucticus ludovicianus

The male Rose-breasted Grosbeak has a voice to match his magnificent plumage, and he flaunts both in treetop performances. Although the female lacks the formal dress of her mate, she shares his musical talents—whether the nest is incubated by the male or the female, the developing young are introduced into the world of song by the brooding parent.

This common songster's boldness does not go unnoticed by the appreciative birding community, which eagerly anticipates the male's annual spring concert in Central Park, Bronx Park and the North Shore Wildlife Sanctuary. New York City birders keen on observing this bird's nesting behavior should be able to find a pair in the pockets of mature deciduous woodlands in Westchester and northern Nassau counties.

The Rose-breasted Grosbeak is one of the few songbirds in which the male does not acquire his full plumage until his second breeding season. First-year males are brown where adults are black, and they usually have less rose color.

Similar Species: Male is distinctive. Female Purple Finch and sparrows are generally smaller.

Quick ID: smaller than a robin; light-colored, conical bill. *Male:* black hood; rose breast; black back and wings; white rump; white wing bars. *Female:* heavily streaked with brown; thin, white eyebrow; light throat.
Size: 7–8 in.

Jan Feb Mar Apr May Jun Jul Aug Sept Oct Nov Dec

Indigo Bunting

Passerina cyanea

♀

breeding

♂

Metallic blue male Indigo Buntings are frequently encountered in open areas of overgrown fields and along forest edges. Perched atop a shrub or thicket, the males conduct elaborate tactical maneuvers with song. With rival males only a voice away, Indigo Buntings call throughout the day, attempting to maintain superiority over their peers. Neighboring males copy and learn from one another, producing 'song territories.' Each male in a song territory adds a personal variation to the basic tune of *fire-fire, where-where, here-here, see-it see-it*, producing his own acoustic fingerprint.

Indigo Buntings are widespread throughout our area during summer, popping out of dense bushes anywhere from Conference House Park on Staten Island to northern Nassau County. They build a small cup nest low to the ground in an upright crotch among a shrubby tangle. Once their nesting duties are complete, these buntings are quick to leave our area, beginning their exodus in September after a partial molt.

Similar Species: Eastern Bluebird (p. 100) is larger and has a red breast and a slimmer body. Female is similar to many sparrows, but they usually have more heavily streaked plumage.

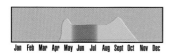

Jan Feb Mar Apr May Jun Jul Aug Sept Oct Nov Dec

Quick ID: sparrow-sized; conical bill. *Male:* turquoise blue plumage; darker wings and tail. *Female:* soft brown overall; hints of blue on rump.
Size: 5¹/₂ in.

House Sparrow
Passer domesticus

This common backyard bird often confuses novice birdwatchers because the females and immatures can be very nondescript. The male is relatively conspicuous—he has a black bib, a gray cap and white lines trailing down from his mouth (as though he has spilled milk on himself)—and he sings a continuous, monotone series of *cheep-cheep-cheep* notes. The best field mark for the female, apart from her pale eyebrows, is that there are no distinctive field marks.

The House Sparrow was first successfully introduced to North America in 1853 at Greenwood Cemetery in Brooklyn with the hope of controlling insect pests. Unfortunately, the majority of its diet is seeds, and it has become somewhat of a pest itself. The House Sparrow's aggressive nature usurps several native songbirds from nesting cavities, and its boldness often drives other birds away from backyard feeders. The House Sparrow and the European Starling, two of the most common birds in New York City and Long Island, are a constant reminder of the negative impact of human introductions on natural systems.

Similar Species: Male is distinctive. Female is similar to female sparrows and finches, but she tends to lack any distinctive markings whatsoever.

Quick ID: mid-sized sparrow; brownish-gray belly. *Male:* black throat; gray forehead; white jowl; chestnut nape. *Female:* plain; unstreaked; pale eyebrow; mottled back and wings.
Size: 5 1/2–6 1/2 in.

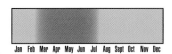

Jan Feb Mar Apr May Jun Jul Aug Sept Oct Nov Dec

WATCHING BIRDS

Identifying your first new bird can be so satisfying that you just might become addicted to birdwatching. Luckily, birdwatching does not have to be expensive. It all hinges on how involved in this hobby you want to get. Setting up a simple backyard feeder is an easy way to get to know the birds sharing your neighborhood, and some people simply find bird-watching a pleasant way to complement a nightly walk with the dog or a morning commute into work.

Many people enjoy going to urban parks and feeding the wild birds that have become accustomed to humans. This activity provides people with intimate contact with urban-dwelling birds, but remember that birdseed, or better yet the birds' natural food items, are much healthier for the birds than bread and crackers.

Seasons of Birdwatching

SPRING

The coming of spring is celebrated by the sights and sounds of migrant birds arriving in our city. The early appearance of the Horned Lark, Red-winged Blackbird, American Robin and Song Sparrow all remind us that warmer days are just around the corner. During April and May, many shorebirds, gulls and terns arrive on our coastal shorelines from distant wintering grounds. At the same time, other species that have wintered here in New York are embarking on travels north to spend the summer months. Day by day the tempo of bird migration escalates. Throughout April and May, warm southwest winds are accompanied by huge flights of landbirds. For a short period, New York's parks and backyards are alive with a bustling of activity as warblers, vireos and flycatchers busily navi-gate their way through our city. May is peak migration time in areas around New York but by the end of the month, our city's woodlands, bays and marshes have come to a migratory standstill; it is time for the serious business of nesting.

SUMMER

New York has a very impressive list of breeding birds, and summer offers many sights for the avid birder. Areas such as Jones Beach State Park, along the south shore of Long Island, are inhabited by colonies of gulls, terns, herons and egrets, and watch for Black Skimmers on the open waters. Jamaica Bay Wildlife Refuge is also an excellent place to visit during these summer months. Although there is relatively less bird activity among our parks, beaches and shorelines during the summer months, rarely a day goes by without movement or change. In July and August many shorebirds are once again retreating south—a sign that fall migration is well on its way.

FALL

Fall migration is a prolonged affair, beginning as early as July and extending well into December. The season commences with the arrival of post-breeding migratory shorebirds to local beaches, bays and tidal flats. September is the time to watch for a mass migration of raptors, a much-anticipated birding event. Broad-winged Hawks often occur in spectacular flights around inland parks while Sharp-shinned Hawks and American Kestrels can be seen in large numbers along coastal shores. Jacob Riis Park in Queens is an exceptional spot to view these natural phenomena. Also in September, warblers and swallows swarm local parks and beaches, followed closely by the arrival of sparrows and kinglets in October. Concentrations of herons, gulls, terns and waterfowl are at their height, tapering off through early November with a concurrent build-up of waterfowl and wintering bird populations. Fall in the New York area is a time of great change and fluctuation in local bird populations because of the almost daily arrival and departure of migrants.

WINTER

Not a day goes by without some movement of birdlife in and around the New
York area. Through particularly cold
winters, many waterfowl move south to
escape the weather, but during mild winters some birds actually make an early return to our city. Winter brings good numbers of birds to backyard feeding stations: White-throated Sparrows, chickadees and Northern Cardinals are common visitors to neighborhood yards and in some years, American Goldfinches can be spotted. Pelham Bay Park on Long Island Sound is an excellent site to watch for wintering water birds, such as mergansers, grebes and common goldeneyes. During mid-winter, watch for cormorants perched on the rocky outcrops of Twin Islands and among the pine and spruce groves of Pelham Bay. An attentive birder might even catch a glimpse of a Great Horned Owl or Eastern Screech-Owl.

Birding Optics

Most people who are interested in bird-watching will eventually buy a pair of binoculars. They help you identify key bird characteristics, such as plumage and bill color, and they also help you identify other birders! Birdwatchers are a friendly sort, and a chat among birders is all part of the experience.

You'll use your binoculars often, so select a pair that will contribute to the quality of your birdwatching experience—they don't have to be expensive. If you need help deciding which pair is right for you, talk to other birdwatchers or to someone at your local nature center. Many models are available, and when shopping for binoculars it's important to keep two things in mind: weight and magnification.

One of the first things you'll notice about binoculars (apart from the price extremes) is that they all have two numbers associated with them (8 x 40, for example). The first number, which is always the smallest, is the magnification (how large the bird will appear); the second number is the size (in millimeters) of the objective lens (the larger end). It might seem important at first to get the highest magnification possible, but a reasonable magnification of seven to eight times is optimal for all-purpose birding, because it draws you fairly close to most birds without causing too much vibration. Some shaking happens to everyone; to overcome it, rest the binoculars against a support, such as a partner's shoulder or a tree.

The size of the objective lens is really a question of birding conditions and weight. Because wider lenses (40–50 mm) will bring in more light, they are preferred for birding in low-light situations (like before sunrise or after sunset). If these aren't the conditions that you will be pursuing, a light pair that has an objective lens diameter of less than 30 mm could be the right choice. Because binoculars tend to feel heavy after hanging around your neck all day, the compact models are becoming increasingly popular. If you have a pair that is heavy, you can purchase a strap that redistributes part of the weight to the shoulders and lower back.

Another valuable piece of equipment is a spotting scope. It is very useful when you are trying to sight waterfowl, shorebirds or soaring raptors, but it is really of no use if you are intent on seeing forest birds. A good spotting scope has a magnification of about 40x. It has a sturdy tripod or a window mount for the car. Be wary of non-birding of telescopes that are designed for seeing stars. Their magnification is too great for bird-watching. One of the advantages of having a scope is that you will be able to see far-off birds, which can help during winter (to see waterfowl overwintering offshore, for example) or during migration (to see shorebirds and raptors). By setting up in one spot (or by not even leaving your car) you can observe faraway flocks that would be little more than specks in your binoculars.

With these simple pieces of equipment (none of which is truly essential) and this handy field guide, anyone can enjoy birds in the New York area. After experiencing the thrill of a couple of hard-won identifications, you will find yourself taking your binoculars on walks, drives and trips to the beach and to the country. As rewards accumulate with experience, you might find the books and photos piling up and your trips being planned just to see birds!

Birding by Ear

Sometimes, bird listening can be more effective than bird watching. Many birds are difficult to see because they stay hidden in treetops, but you can learn to identify them by their songs. The technique of birding by ear is gaining popularity, because listening for birds can be more efficient, productive and rewarding than waiting for a visual confirmation. Birds have distinctive songs that they use to resolve territorial disputes, and sound is therefore a useful way to identify species. It is particularly useful when trying to watch some of the smaller forest-dwelling birds. Their size and often indistinct plumage can make a visual search of the forest canopy frustrating. To facilitate auditory searches, catchy paraphrases are included in the descriptions of many of the birds. If the paraphrase just doesn't seem to work for you (they are often a personal thing) be creative and try to find one that fits. By spending time playing the song over in your head, fitting words to it, the voices of birds soon become as familiar as the voices of family members. Many excellent CDs and tapes are available at bookstores and wild-bird stores for the songs of the birds in your area.

Birdfeeders

They're messy, they can be costly, and they're sprouting up in neighborhoods everywhere. Feeding birds has become a common pastime in residential communities all over North America. Although the concept is fairly straightforward, as with anything else involving birds, feeders can become quite elaborate.

The great advantage to feeding birds is that neighborhood chickadees, jays, juncos and finches are enticed into regular visits. Don't expect birds to arrive at your feeder as soon as you set it up; it can take weeks for a few regulars to incorporate your yard into their daily routine. As the popularity of your feeder grows, the number of visiting birds will increase and more species will arrive. You will notice that your feeder is busier during the winter months, when natural foods are less abundant. You can increase the odds of a good avian turnout by using a variety of feeders and seeds. When a number of birds habitually visit your yard, maintaining the feeder becomes a responsibility, because the birds might begin to rely on it as a regular food source.

Larger birds tend to enjoy feeding on platforms or on the ground; smaller birds are comfortable on hanging seed dispensers. Certain seeds tend to attract specific birds; nature centers and wild-bird supply stores are the best places to ask how to attract a favorite species. It's mainly seed-eaters that are attracted to backyards; some birds have no interest in feeders. Only the most committed birdwatcher will try to attract birds that are insect eaters, berry eaters or, in some extreme cases, scavengers!

The location of the feeder can influence the amount of business it receives from the neighborhood birds. Because birds are wild, they are instinctively wary, and they are unlikely to visit an area where they might come under attack. When putting up your feeder, think like a bird. A good, clear view with convenient escape routes is always appreciated. Cats like birdfeeders that are close to the ground and within pouncing distance from a bush; obviously, birds don't. Above all, a birdfeeder should be in view of a favorite window, where you can sit and enjoy the rewarding interaction of your appreciative feathered guests.

GLOSSARY

accipiter: a forest hawk (genus *Accipiter*); characterized by a long tail and short, rounded wings; feeds mostly on birds.

brood: *n.* a family of young from one hatching; *v.* sit on eggs so as to hatch them.

conifer: a cone-producing tree, usually a softwood evergreen (e.g., spruce, pine, fir).

corvid: a member of the crow family (Corvidae); includes crows, jays, magpies and ravens.

covey: a brood or flock of partridges, quails or grouse.

crop: an enlargement of the esophagus; serves as a storage structure and (in doves) has glands that produce secretions.

dabbling: a foraging technique used by ducks, where the head and neck are submerged but the body and tail remain on the water's surface; dabbling ducks can usually walk easily on land, can take off without running and have brightly colored speculums.

deciduous tree: a tree that loses its leaves annually (e.g., oak, maple, aspen, birch).

dimorphism: the existence of two distinct forms of a species, such as between the sexes.

eclipse: the dull, female-like plumage that male ducks briefly acquire after molting from their breeding plumage.

elbow patch: a dark spot at the bend of the outstretched wing, seen from below.

flycatching: a feeding behavior where the bird leaves a perch, snatches an insect in mid-air and returns to the same perch; also known as 'hawking' or 'sallying.'

fledgling: a young chick that has just acquired its permanent flight feathers but is still dependent on its parents.

flushing: a behavior where frightened birds explode into flight in response to a disturbance.

gape: the size of the mouth opening.

irruption: a sporadic mass migration of birds into a non-breeding area.

larva: a development stage of an animal (usually an invertebrate) that has a different body form from the adult (e.g., caterpillar, maggot).

leading edge: the front edge of the wing as viewed from below.

litter: fallen plant material, such as twigs, leaves and needles, that forms a distinct layer above the soil, especially in forests.

lore: the small patch between the eye and the bill.

molting: the periodic replacement of worn out feathers (usually twice a year).

morphology: the science of form and shape.

nape: the back of the neck.

neotropical migrant: a bird that nests in North America but overwinters in the New World tropics.

niche: an ecological role filled by a species.

open country: a landscape that is primarily not forested.

parasitism: a relationship between two species where one benefits at the expense of the other.

phylogenetics: a method of classifying organisms that puts together groups that share a common ancestry.

pishing: making a sound to attract birds by saying *pishhh* as loudly and as wetly as possible.

polygynous: having a mating strategy where one male breeds with several females.

polyandrous: having a mating strategy where one female breeds with several males.

plucking post: a perch habitually used by a raptor for plucking feathers from its prey.

raptor: a carnivorous (meat-eating) bird; includes eagles, hawks, falcons and owls.

rufous: rusty red in color.

speculum: a brightly colored patch in the wings of many dabbling ducks.

squeaking: making a sound to attract birds by loudly kissing the back of the hand, or by using a specially design squeaky bird call.

talons: the claws of birds of prey.

understory: the shrub or thicket layer beneath a canopy of trees.

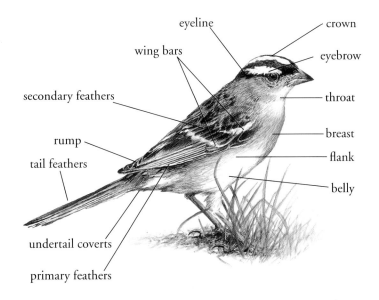

eyeline   crown

wing bars   eyebrow

secondary feathers   throat

rump   breast

tail feathers   flank

belly

undertail coverts

primary feathers

REFERENCES

American Ornithologists' Union. 1983–97. *Check-list of North American Birds*. 6th ed. (and supplements). American Ornithologists' Union, Washington, D.C.

Andrle, R., and J. R. Carroll. 1988. *The Atlas of Breeding Birds in New York State*. Cornell University Press, Ithaca.

Birdwatchers of Central Park. 1995. *The Birds of Central Park: An Annotated Checklist*. Central Park Conservancy, New York.

Bull, J. 1964. *Birds of the New York Area*. Dover Publications, New York.

Davis, T. H. 1994. *Birds of the Jamaica Bay Wildlife Refuge* [checklist]. U.S. Department of the Interior, National Park Service, Gateway National Recreation Area, New York.

DeGraaf, R. M., and J. H. Rappole. 1995. *Neotropical Migratory Birds: Natural History, Distribution, and Population Change*. Cornell University Press, Ithaca.

Drennan, S. R. 1981. *Where to Find Birds in New York State*. Syracuse University Press, New York.

Ehrlich, P. R., D. S. Dobkin and D. Wheye. 1988. *The Birder's Handbook*. Fireside, New York.

Evans, H. E. 1993. *Pioneer Naturalists: The Discovery and Naming of North American Plants and Animals*. Henry Holt and Company, New York.

Farrand, J., ed. 1983. *The Audubon Society Master Guide to Birding*. 3 vols. Alfred A. Knopf, New York.

Federation of New York State Bird Clubs. 1996. *Checklist of the Birds of New York State*. Ithaca.

Gotch, A. F. 1981. *Birds: Their Latin Names Explained*. Blandford Press, Dorset, England.

Griggs, J. L. 1997. *American Bird Conservancy's Field Guide to All the Birds of North America*. Harper Collins Publishers, New York.

Jones, J. O. 1990. *Where the Birds Are: A Guide to All 50 States and Canada*. William Morrow and Company, New York.

Kaufmann, K. 1996. *Lives of North American Birds*. Houghton Mifflin Company, New York.

Mearns, B., and R. Mearns. 1992. *Audubon to Xantus: The Lives of Those Commemorated in North American Bird Names*. Academic Press, San Diego.

National Audubon Society. 1971–95. *American Birds*. Vols. 25–48.

Pettingill, O. S., Jr. 1977. *A Guide to Bird Finding East of the Mississippi*. Oxford University Press, New York.

Reader's Digest Association. *Book of North American Birds*. The Reader's Digest Association, Pleasantville, N.Y.

Robbins, C. S., B. Bruun and H. S. Zim. 1966. *Birds of North America*. Golden Press, New York.

Scott, S. S. 1987. *Field Guide to the Birds of North America*. National Geographic Society, Washington, D.C.

Terres, J. K. 1995. *The Audubon Society Encyclopedia of North American Birds*. Wings Books, New York.

CHECKLIST OF NEW YORK CITY & WESTERN LONG ISLAND BIRDS

This checklist includes 308 bird species recorded in New York City, western Long Island and the surrounding ocean habitats. It was compiled using *The Atlas of Breeding Birds in New York State* (Andrle and Carroll 1988), *Birds of the New York Area* (Bull 1964), *Where to Find Birds in New York State* (Drennan 1981), *Where the Birds Are* (Jones 1990), *The Birds of Central Park: An Annotated Checklist* (Central Park Conservancy 1995) and *Birds of the Jamaica Bay Wildlife Refuge* (Davis 1994).

CHECKLIST SYMBOLS

Seasons

W	=	Winter (mid-December through February)
Sp	=	Spring (March through May)
Su	=	Summer (June through July)
F	=	Fall (August through early December)

Breeding Status

B	=	Regular breeder (nests every year)
b	=	Irregular breeder (nests infrequently; few nesting records)
?	=	Suspected breeder (no confirmation of nesting)
+	=	Former breeder (no nesting records in recent years)
L	=	Local breeder (restricted to a few locations)

Abundance (in appropriate habitats)

C	=	Common to abundant (always present in large numbers)
F	=	Fairly common (always present in moderate to small numbers)
U	=	Uncommon (usually present in small numbers)
R	=	Rare (observed in very small numbers, and perhaps not every year)
X	=	Extremely rare (fewer than 10 recorded sightings during that season)
-	=	Absent (no recorded sightings)
e	=	Erratic (can occur in substantially larger or smaller numbers during certain years)
*	=	Abundant offshore (pelagic)

The species in this checklist are listed in taxonomic order (in accordance with the 41st supplement [July 1997] of the American Ornithologists' Union's *Check-list of North American Birds*). A blank line separates each family of birds. This checklist does not include 'accidental' species (recorded fewer than 10 times ever in our area).

	W	Sp	Su	F
❑ Red-throated Loon	F	C	-	C
❑ Common Loon	U	F	X	F
❑ Pied-billed Grebe (BL)	U	U	R	F
❑ Horned Grebe	F	C	X	C
❑ Red-necked Grebe	R	R	-	R
❑ Cory's Shearwater	-	-	-	R*
❑ Greater Shearwater	-	R*	R*	-
❑ Sooty Shearwater	-	R*	R*	-
❑ Wilson's Storm-Petrel	-	-	U*	-
❑ Northern Gannet	R*	U*	X*	U*
❑ Great Cormorant	C	U	R	U
❑ Double-crested Cormorant (BL)	R*	C	U	C
❑ American Bittern (+)	U	U	R	U
❑ Least Bittern (BL)	-	R	R	R
❑ Great Blue Heron	U	F	U	F
❑ Great Egret (BL)	X	F	F	F
❑ Snowy Egret (BL)	-	F	F	F
❑ Little Blue Heron (BL)	X	U	U	U
❑ Tricolored Heron (BL)	X	U	U	U
❑ Cattle Egret (BL)	-	U	U	U
❑ Green Heron (B)	-	F	U	F
❑ Black-crowned Night-Heron (BL)	U	F	F	F
❑ Yellow-crowned Night-Heron (BL)	-	U	U	U
❑ Glossy Ibis (BL)	-	F	F	F
❑ Turkey Vulture	R	F	R	F
❑ Tundra Swan	R-	-	R	
❑ Mute Swan (B)	F	F	F	F
❑ Snow Goose	R	Ue	X	Ue
❑ Brant	C	C	C	C
❑ Canada Goose (B)	C	C	C	C
❑ Wood Duck (B)	R	U	R	U
❑ Green-winged Teal (b)	U	C	R	C
❑ American Black Duck (B)	C	C	C	C
❑ Mallard (B)	C	C	C	C
❑ Northern Pintail	U	F	X	F
❑ Blue-winged Teal (b)	X	F	R	C
❑ Northern Shoveler (b)	U	F	R	U
❑ Gadwall (B)	F	F	F	F
❑ Eurasian Wigeon	R	R	-	R
❑ American Wigeon	C	C	X	C
❑ Canvasback	U	R	-	F
❑ Redhead (b)	R	R	X	R
❑ Ring-necked Duck	R	U	-	U
❑ Greater Scaup	C	C	R	C
❑ Lesser Scaup	U	U	X	U
❑ Common Eider	R	-	-	-
❑ King Eider	R	-	-	-
❑ Harlequin Duck	R	-	-	-
❑ Oldsquaw	U	U	-	U
❑ Black Scoter	U	U	X	U
❑ Surf Scoter	U	U	-	U
❑ White-winged Scoter	U	U	-	U
❑ Common Goldeneye	F	F	-	F

	W	Sp	Su	F
❑ Bufflehead	C	C	X	C
❑ Hooded Merganser	U	U	X	U
❑ Common Merganser	R	R	-	R
❑ Red-breasted Merganser	C	C	X	C
❑ Ruddy Duck (BL)	U	U	U	U
❑ Osprey (BL)	X	U	R	F
❑ Bald Eagle	R	-	R	R
❑ Northern Harrier (BL)	F	F	U	C
❑ Sharp-shinned Hawk (+)	U	U	X	C
❑ Cooper's Hawk	R	R	-	U
❑ Northern Goshawk	R	R	-	R
❑ Red-shouldered Hawk (+)	R	R	-	R
❑ Broad-winged Hawk (BL)	-	F	R	C
❑ Red-tailed Hawk (B)	F	F	R	C
❑ Rough-legged Hawk	Re	-	-	Re
❑ American Kestrel (B)	U	U	U	C
❑ Merlin	R	R	-	U
❑ Peregrine Falcon (BL)	R	R	R	U
❑ Gyrfalcon	X	-	-	X
❑ Ring-necked Pheasant (B)	R	R	R	R
❑ Northern Bobwhite (BL)	U	U	U	U
❑ Black Rail (b)	-	X	X	X
❑ Clapper Rail (BL)	R	R	R	R
❑ King Rail	-	X	X	X
❑ Virginia Rail (BL)	R	R	R	R
❑ Sora (BL)	-	X	R	R
❑ Common Moorhen (BL)	-	R	R	R
❑ American Coot (BL)	R	U	R	U
❑ Black-bellied Plover	U	C	U	C
❑ American Golden-Plover	-	R	X	U
❑ Semipalmated Plover	R	C	C	C
❑ Piping Plover (BL)	-	R	R	R
❑ Killdeer (B)	R	C	C	C
❑ American Oystercatcher (BL)	R	U	U	U
❑ Greater Yellowlegs	R	F	U	C
❑ Lesser Yellowlegs	X	C	F	C
❑ Solitary Sandpiper	-	U	-	U
❑ Willet (B)	-	C	C	C
❑ Spotted Sandpiper (B)	F	F	F	F
❑ Upland Sandpiper (BL)	-	R	R	R
❑ Whimbrel	-	R	X	R
❑ Hudsonian Godwit	-	-	R	R
❑ Marbled Godwit	-	X	R	R
❑ Ruddy Turnstone	R	U	R	U
❑ Red Knot	R	U	R	U
❑ Sanderling	U	U	R	U
❑ Semipalmated Sandpiper	-	C	U	C
❑ Western Sandpiper	R	F	U	C
❑ Least Sandpiper	-	C	U	C
❑ White-rumped Sandpiper	-	C	U	C
❑ Baird's Sandpiper	-	-	-	R
❑ Pectoral Sandpiper	-	U	R	F
❑ Purple Sandpiper	F	U	-	U
❑ Dunlin	F	C	R	C

	W	Sp	Su	F
❑ Curlew Sandpiper	-	X	X	X
❑ Stilt Sandpiper	-	R	X	U
❑ Buff-breasted Sandpiper	-	-	-	R
❑ Ruff/Reeve	-	R	R	R
❑ Short-billed Dowitcher	X	C	F	C
❑ Long-billed Dowitcher	X	R	R	U
❑ Common Snipe	R	U	-	U
❑ American Woodcock (BL)	X	U	U	U
❑ Wilson's Phalarope	-	R	-	R
❑ Red-necked Phalarope	-	R	-	R
❑ Red Phalarope	-	R*	-	R*
❑ Pomarine Jaeger	-	R*	-	R*
❑ Parasitic Jaeger	-	R*	-	R*
❑ Laughing Gull (BL)	-	C	C	C
❑ Little Gull	R	X	X	X
❑ Black-headed Gull	R	X	X	X
❑ Bonaparte's Gull	F	F	R	F
❑ Ring-billed Gull	C	C	U	C
❑ Herring Gull (BL)	C	C	C	C
❑ Iceland Gull	R	X	-	X
❑ Lesser Black-backed Gull	X	X	-	X
❑ Glaucous Gull	R	X	-	X
❑ Great Black-backed Gull (BL)	C	C	C	C
❑ Black-legged Kittiwake	R*	-	-	R*
❑ Gull-billed Tern (b)	-	R	R	R
❑ Caspian Tern	-	R	R	U
❑ Royal Tern	-	R	R	U
❑ Roseate Tern (BL)	-	U	U	R
❑ Common Tern (BL)	-	C	F	C
❑ Forster's Tern (b)	-	U	U	C
❑ Least Tern (BL)	-	U	U	R
❑ Black Tern	-	R	R	R
❑ Black Skimmer (BL)	-	F	F	F
❑ Rock Dove (B)	C	C	C	C
❑ Mourning Dove (B)	C	C	C	C
❑ Black-billed Cuckoo (BL)	-	Re	Re	Re
❑ Yellow-billed Cuckoo (BL)	-	Re	Re	Re
❑ Barn Owl (BL)	R	R	R	R
❑ Eastern Screech-Owl (BL)	R	R	R	R
❑ Great Horned Owl (BL)	R	R	R	R
❑ Snowy Owl	Re	-	-	-
❑ Barred Owl	X	X	X	X
❑ Long-eared Owl (+)	R	X	X	X
❑ Short-eared Owl (BL)	R	R	R	R
❑ Northern Saw-whet Owl (BL)	R	R	R	R
❑ Common Nighthawk (BL)	-	R	R	U
❑ Chuck-will's-widow (b)	-	-	R	-
❑ Whip-poor-will (+)	-	R	R	R
❑ Chimney Swift (B)	-	C	C	C
❑ Ruby-throated Hummingbird	-	U	R	U
❑ Belted Kingfisher (B)	R	U	R	U

	W	Sp	Su	F
❑ Red-headed Woodpecker	R	R	X	R
❑ Red-bellied Woodpecker (B)	R	R	R	R
❑ Yellow-bellied Sapsucker	-	R	-	U
❑ Downy Woodpecker (B)	C	C	C	C
❑ Hairy Woodpecker (B)	U	U	U	U
❑ Northern Flicker (B)	U	F	U	C
❑ Pileated Woodpecker	X	X	X	X
❑ Olive-sided Flycatcher	-	R	-	U
❑ Eastern Wood-Pewee (BL)	-	F	F	F
❑ Yellow-bellied Flycatcher	-	R	-	R
❑ Acadian Flycatcher (?)	-	R	R	R
❑ Alder Flycatcher	-	R	-	R
❑ Willow Flycatcher (B)	-	U	U	-
❑ Least Flycatcher	-	U	R	U
❑ Eastern Phoebe (B)	-	C	R	C
❑ Great Crested Flycatcher (B)	-	F	F	F
❑ Western Kingbird	-	-	-	R
❑ Eastern Kingbird (B)	-	F	F	F
❑ Northern Shrike	Re	R	-	R
❑ Loggerhead Shrike	X	X	-	R
❑ White-eyed Vireo (BL)	-	U	U	U
❑ Blue-headed Vireo	-	U	-	U
❑ Yellow-throated Vireo (BL)	-	U	R	U
❑ Warbling Vireo (B)	-	U	R	U
❑ Philadelphia Vireo	-	R	-	R
❑ Red-eyed Vireo (B)	-	F	F	F
❑ Blue Jay (B)	F	F	U	C
❑ American Crow (B)	C	C	C	C
❑ Fish Crow (B)	F	F	F	F
❑ Horned Lark (B)	U	U	U	U
❑ Purple Martin (BL)	-	R	R	R
❑ Tree Swallow (B)	R	C	F	C
❑ Northern Rough-winged Swallow (B)	-	R	U	R
❑ Bank Swallow (BL)	-	R	U	R
❑ Cliff Swallow	-	R	-	R
❑ Barn Swallow (B)	-	C	C	C
❑ Black-capped Chickadee (B)	C	C	C	C
❑ Boreal Chickadee	Xe	Xe	-	Xe
❑ Tufted Titmouse (B)	F	F	F	F
❑ Red-breasted Nuthatch (BL)	Re	Re	Re	Re
❑ White-breasted Nuthatch (B)	U	U	U	U
❑ Brown Creeper (BL)	R	U	R	U
❑ Carolina Wren (B)	R	R	R	R
❑ House Wren (B)	-	F	F	F
❑ Winter Wren	R	R	-	R
❑ Sedge Wren	-	X	-	X
❑ Marsh Wren (BL)	R	U	U	U

	W	Sp	Su	F
Golden-crowned Kinglet	Re	U	-	C
Ruby-crowned Kinglet	R	U	-	C
Blue-gray Gnatcatcher (BL)	-	U	R	R
Eastern Bluebird (BL)	R	R	R	R
Veery (B)	-	U	R	C
Gray-cheeked Thrush	-	R	-	R
Swainson's Thrush	-	R	-	U
Hermit Thrush (BL)	R	F	X	F
Wood Thrush (B)	-	U	U	U
American Robin (B)	Ue	C	C	C
European Starling (B)	C	C	C	C
Gray Catbird (B)	R	F	F	F
Northern Mockingbird (B)	F	F	F	F
Brown Thrasher (B)	R	U	R	U
American Pipit	R	R	-	U
Cedar Waxwing (BL)	Re	F	R	F
Blue-winged Warbler (BL)	-	F	R	U
Golden-winged Warbler	-	R	-	R
Tennessee Warbler	-	U	-	U
Orange-crowned Warbler	Xe	R	-	R
Nashville Warbler	-	U	-	U
Northern Parula	-	U	-	U
Yellow Warbler (B)	-	F	U	F
Chestnut-sided Warbler (BL)	-	U	R	U
Magnolia Warbler	-	U	-	U
Cape May Warbler	-	U	-	F
Black-throated Blue Warbler	-	U	-	F
Yellow-rumped Warbler	Re	C	-	C
Black-throated Green Warbler	-	F	-	F
Blackburnian Warbler	-	U	-	U
Yellow-throated Warbler	X	R	-	R
Pine Warbler	X	R	-	R
Prairie Warbler (BL)	-	U	R	U
Palm Warbler	X	F	-	F
Bay-breasted Warbler	-	U	-	U
Blackpoll Warbler	-	U	-	F
Cerulean Warbler	-	R	X	R
Black-and-white Warbler (BL)	-	F	R	F
American Redstart (BL)	-	C	R	C
Prothonotary Warbler	-	R	-	X
Worm-eating Warbler (?)	-	R	R	R
Ovenbird (BL)	-	F	R	F
Northern Waterthrush	-	U	-	F
Louisiana Waterthrush (?)	-	R	R	R
Kentucky Warbler (b)	-	R	R	R
Connecticut Warbler	-	-	-	R
Mourning Warbler	-	R	-	R
Common Yellowthroat (B)	X	C	C	C
Hooded Warbler	-	R	R	R
Wilson's Warbler	-	R	-	R
Canada Warbler	-	U	-	U
Yellow-breasted Chat (BL)	R	R	R	R
Summer Tanager	-	R	-	R
Scarlet Tanager (B)	-	F	R	F
Eastern Towhee (B)	R	F	F	F
American Tree Sparrow	F	R	-	F
Chipping Sparrow (B)	R	U	U	U
Clay-colored Sparrow	-	-	-	R
Field Sparrow (BL)	R	U	U	U
Vesper Sparrow	R	R	-	R
Lark Sparrow	-	X	-	R
Savannah Sparrow (BL)	U	U	R	U
Grasshopper Sparrow (B)	-	R	R	R
Henslow's Sparrow	-	X	-	X
Nelson's Sharp-tailed Sparrow	-	U	-	U
Saltmarsh Sharp-tailed Sparrow (BL)	X	R	R	R
Seaside Sparrow (BL)	X	R	R	R
Fox Sparrow	R	R	-	U
Song Sparrow (BL)	R	F	F	C
Lincoln's Sparrow	-	R	-	R
Swamp Sparrow (B)	R	R	R	U
White-throated Sparrow (?)	F	F	X	C
White-crowned Sparrow	R	R	-	R
Dark-eyed Junco	U	U	-	C
Lapland Longspur	R	-	-	R
Snow Bunting	U	-	-	R
Northern Cardinal (B)	C	C	C	C
Rose-breasted Grosbeak (B)	-	F	R	F
Blue Grosbeak (b)	-	R	X	R
Indigo Bunting (B)	-	U	U	U
Dickcissel	X	X	-	R
Bobolink (?)	-	R	X	C
Red-winged Blackbird (B)	C	C	C	C
Eastern Meadowlark (BL)	X	R	R	R
Rusty Blackbird	R	R	-	R
Boat-tailed Grackle (bL)	R	R	R	R
Common Grackle (B)	U	C	C	C
Brown-headed Cowbird (B)	U	F	F	F
Orchard Oriole (BL)	-	R	R	-
Baltimore Oriole (B)	-	F	U	F
Pine Grosbeak	Xe	-	-	Xe
Purple Finch	Ue	Ue	-	U
House Finch (B)	C	C	C	C
Red Crossbill	Re	-	-	Rre
White-winged Crossbill	Re	-	-	Re
Common Redpoll	Re	-	-	Re
Pine Siskin (b)	Ue	Re	-	Ue
American Goldfinch (B)	U	U	U	F
Evening Grosbeak	Re	Re	-	Re
House Sparrow (B)	C	C	C	C

INDEX OF SCIENTIFIC NAMES

This index references only the primary, illustrated species descriptions.

INDEX OF COMMON NAMES

Pages numbers in boldface type refer to primary, illustrated species descriptions.

About the Authors

When he's not out watching birds, frogs or snakes, Chris Fisher researches endangered species management and wildlife interpretation at the University of Alberta in Edmonton and serves as president of the local Natural History Club. Chris has traveled throughout North America and Southeast Asia in pursuit of wild places, and he has produced a series of acclaimed bird guides. By sharing his enthusiasm and passion for wild things through lectures, photographs and articles, Chris strives to foster a greater appreciation for the value of our wilderness.

Inspired by wild creatures and wild places, Andy Bezener has developed a keen interest in the study and conservation of birds. Field work with the Canadian Wildlife Service, in addition to studies at Lethbridge Community College and the University of Alberta, has given Andy joyful insight into the lives of many North American birds. His passion and concern for wilderness and wildlife has led him across much of the continent, from the eastern United States to the Queen Charlotte Islands, and from southeastern Arizona to Victoria Island, N.W.T. Through photography, writing, public speaking and travel, he continues to search for a deeper understanding and more meaningful appreciation of nature.